Frary, Dave.
    222 tips for building model railroad
structures / by Dave Frary ; photos by
the author. -- Waukesha, WI : Kalmbach
Books, 1992.
    63 p. : ill. ; 28 cm. -- (Model
railroad handbook ; no. 34)
    ISBN 0-89024-145-7

    1. Railroads--Models. I. Title II.
Title: Two hundred twenty-two tips for
building model railroad structures.
III. Series

InKo   14 DEC 93   26129045   IKPAsl   92-22782r92

222 TIPS
FOR BUILDING MODEL RAILROAD STRUCTURES

MODEL RAILROAD HANDBOOK NO. 34

BY DAVE FRARY   PHOTOS BY THE AUTHOR

KALMBACH **K** BOOKS®

First printing, 1992. Second printing, 1993.

Originally published in 1989 by Blue Ribbon Models.

Frary, Dave.
    222 Tips for building model railroad structures / Dave Frary.
        p.   cm.
    Includes index
    ISBN 0-89024-145-7
    1. Railroads—Models. I. Title. II. Title: Two hundred twenty-
two tips for building model railroad structures.
TF197.F677 1992
625. 1'9—dc20   92-22782

Introduction

THIS BOOK IS a collection of my favorite structure-building tips and modeling techniques, techniques developed during more than 30 years of craftsman kit building. Some of the tips will help you as you start a modeling project; others will help you through complicated building steps. And many others provide painting, finishing, and detailing techniques to help you show off all your hard work to best advantage.

GETTING STARTED WITH CRAFTSMAN KITS

Plastic kits can provide every nut and bolt — even simulated wood grain — but they can't provide the invisible item that comes in the box with most craftsman kits: real modeling satisfaction. That's exactly what craftsman kits are about.

If you're reading this book you've probably already sampled craftsman-type kits. If you haven't, these slightly more complex kits will open a whole new world of modeling pleasure for you. There's a lot of gratification in taking a box full of wood sticks, metal or plastic castings, cardboard, and sundry other materials and assembling them into an attractive model — one that won't fit back in the box!

Even if you don't have the space (or the urge) to build a layout right now, you can have a lot of fun and "bank time," by building a closet full of craftsman structures, saving them until the day when you can plunk them down on your layout.

YOUR FIRST CRAFTSMAN STRUCTURE

The first craftsman kit you build shouldn't be your largest or most expensive. Instead, choose a small project, and if you're in the mood for advice, choose the smallest Campbell kit that you like. The reason for this is the instructions. Campbell instructions have been among the best craftsman kit directions for as long as I can remember. They will get you going and keep you going with out undue beginner frustration.

After you've completed a simple Campbell kit move on to a bigger project, one that will continue building your confidence and introduce you to more advanced construction and finishing techniques. Every craftsman kit will teach you new techniques — soon you'll be a pro, making up and refining your own techniques as you continue to build. Before long, I'll be reading your book!

JUST A LITTLE MODELING PHILOSOPHY

As you build more and more craftsman-type kits you'll develop a personal set of rules to apply to all your structures. Everybody has a different philosophy, just as everyone builds kits differently. The rules I follow result from a desire to build complete scenes that capture the look and feel of prototype scenes: Often my models are more caricature than board-by-board copies of the real thing. My nine rules are:

❶ Don't be afraid to depart from the instructions when you've got a good reason to do so
❷ Model only what you can see
❸ Don't spend time on interior detail except window curtains and shades
❹ Structure models don't have to be exact
❺ Think of your models in terms of the scenes they will be part of, not as individual buildings
❻ Don't worry if everything doesn't turn out perfect
❼ Don't use same set of techniques on every structure
❽ Weather everything (but not the same way)
❾ Above all, try to capture the flavor of the structure and its surroundings.

HOW TO USE THIS BOOK

I've organized and indexed this book so it can serve as your general kit-building reference. It's a tool to help you build models better, and that means it's not meant to be read from cover to cover like a novel. Instead, it's a book for thumbing and browsing and ready reference. For example, if you're starting a wood kit with plastic doors and windows and the instructions tell you to paint the windows first, look up "Window and door castings" and "Painting plastic" in the index, and see if you can use some of my techniques to make the job easier.

I hope you enjoy this book — and I hope you'll use it to have more fun building structures.

DAVE

Dave Frary

(Left) Pete Laier's HO Arcadia Northern featured a superb mix of craftsman-type and plastic structures, as well as a healthy dollop of eye-catching waterfront atmosphere.

This HO Builders In Scale fishing shanty was assembled with just a handful of common tools.

1
Getting started with the right tools

IF YOU'RE A NEWCOMER to craftsman kit building, you'll need to gather a few tools and set up a work area. Old hands may also want to read this section to check out the tools and techniques we use for our kit projects. Here are suggestions and tips for building a better work place.

LIGHTING

Your work area can be as fancy as a custom-built shop or as simple as the kitchen table, but it should be comfortable, with adequate ventilation and lots of even, glare-free light. Two 40-watt fluorescent tubes in a reflective holder placed about four feet above your work surface provide the minimum light you need for most activities. Some modelers use a high-intensity incandescent desk lamp along with the fluorescent to concentrate more light on their work and some yellow light for color balance.

For model building on the kitchen table I prefer

two high-intensity lamps placed about 18" above and to the side of my work area.

VENTILATION

More and more bad things are being discovered about the adhesives, paints, and solvents we use — and not just in modeling. That makes good ventilation an absolute must.

My shop has an old through-the-wall kitchen exhaust fan mounted in a cellar window over the workbench to suck away noxious fumes. Another simple alternative is a used range hood, but by far the best arrangement for painting is a powerful exhaust fan attached to a custom-built paint booth. The important thing is to evacuate the fumes away from your work area to the outside.

For the kitchen-table workbench select only adhesives, paints and cleaners that are labeled non-toxic. If you must use solvent-based products, a small fan blowing across your work surface or even an open window provides some small measure of safety.

ELECTRICAL OUTLETS

You can use several grounded and fused plug strips around the workbench. An outlet with a built-in light dimmer is cheap and handy for controlling the temperature of soldering irons, wood-burning tools, and even the speed of light motor tools.

GLASS AND WEIGHTS

Among the handiest items you can have on your workbench are a sheet of glass and an assortment of weights. The glass provides an excellent work surface which, besides being flat and true, is perfect for cutting and scribing. Most glues won't stick to glass (a few will, but not anything like they stick to cardstock). The weights are a must for holding just-glued

parts in alignment and to keep your work flat.

My favorite work surface is a 12" x 18" sheet of plate glass. The edges are covered with duct tape to prevent cuts. Instructions and templates are placed under the glass to keep paint and glue from sticking to them, and your hobby knife from cutting them.

On the kitchen table I place the glass over a flattened evening newspaper. It's about the right thick-

ness to protect the table.

The weights serve as flexible holding and positioning jigs. Mine come from all sources, but the fanciest are Miller 90-degree steel machinist's setup blocks.

MAKING AND USING WEIGHTS

Unless you've got more than two hands, about the most helpful thing you can have on your workbench is a good assortment of weights. Weights are useful for holding assemblies while the glue dries, for set-

ting up one-time jigs and fixtures, and even for holding instruction sheets taut and flat.

I've accumulated weights of all shapes and sizes over the years, but here are three kinds that are particularly useful:

❑ If you live near the water, visit a fishing tackle store and size up their surf-casting weights. Anything from 8 ounces on up is extremely handy.

❑ Get out your Yellow Pages and make a few phone calls to find out who sells metal bar stock in your area (if you're stumped, call a few of the firms listed under "Ornamental ironwork" and ask for leads). Eventually, you'll find somebody who sells 1", 1-1/2"-, and 2"-square brass bar, and if you're lucky you'll find a dealer who has a scrap bin of odds and ends that he sells by the pound. I used a hacksaw to cut a dozen or so 3"-long pieces of square bar, trued up the ends with large files, and they're the handiest weights I have.

❑ Ask the service manager where you have your car fixed to save a bucket of old lead tire-balancing weights and battery clamps for you. Heat up a tuna fish can on your stove (do this outdoors if you can), then start melting the tire weights and clamps in it until the can is nearly full. Fish out the non-lead fittings with pliers, then remove the can from the heat. Let cool, strip off the can, file off the sludge on the top, and polish the weight with a Brillo pad for use. These "lead cakes" are the best spare hands you'll ever find during assembly.

STYROFOAM UNIVERSAL HOLDING FIXTURES

A few pieces of thick Styrofoam make handy tool holders on your workbench. Drill, punch or melt holes and slots to organize all sorts of tools, even partially built models.

The Styrofoam can be glued to your bench with white glue to keep it from tipping if tools make it top heavy. Because you can get Styrofoam packaging material or insulation scraps for free, the holding fixtures can be altered or discarded after they have served their purpose. Choose the dense, extruded

type of Styrofoam that is used for house insulation and stay away from the molded stuff that looks like pressed bubbles: It's not as strong.

THE BASIC CRAFTSMAN KIT TOOLBOX

If you're just starting out with craftsman kits, here are the tools you'll need:

❑ **Hobby knives.** I'll bet I must own several dozen hobby knives from half a dozen different makers, but my favorite remains the straight-handled No. 1 X-Acto knife with a No. 11 blade. The only modification you need to make is to wrap the top of the handle with masking tape to make a square or triangular knob. This will keep the knife from rolling off your work surface.

Having a really sharp blade in your hobby knife is always important, and especially critical for cutting Strathmore or other cardboard. Some modelers like to break the old tip from the blade with pliers to produce a new, sharp cutting edge. Others re-sharpen the blade with a small abrasive stone, but both these

methods produce a tip that is inferior to a new blade.

The trick is simple: replace the blade frequently, and spend your time shopping for bargains on blades

instead of trying to make dull blades last! I buy 100-blade bulk packs of No. 11 blades; in 1988 the cost per blade was about 12 cents. The X-Acto bulk packs are available in hobby shops, art-supply stores, some hardware stores, and through hobby tool catalogs.

Art and stationery stores sell battery-operated tip grinders made specially for No. 11 X-Acto blades. These grinders allow you re-sharpen the blade tip dozens of times. If you're an active modeler and are happy with the reground blades, the grinder will pay for itself quickly.

Another handy type of knife for kit building is the Olfa knife, which consists of a handle with a long blade that is scored so it can be broken off to renew

the tip. Olfa was the original brand; there are now several others, and you'll often find them labeled "wallpaper knives." The break-off blade feature makes these knives particularly good for working with heavy cardboard.

❑ **Razor blades.** Single-edge razor blades are preferred by many professional model builders. You can usually find industrial-grade razor blades at hardware or art-supply stores, packaged in boxes of 100. They can't replace modeling knives for some operations, but they cost a lot less, about 5 cents each. Also, they're actually handier than a knife for certain cutting tasks, like chopping stripwood, because they can produce a true, square cut every time.

❑ **Razor saws.** Razor saws are miniature back saws, perfect for cutting wood, plastic and metal. Buy good ones with replaceable blades (Zona is the original), and they will last nearly forever. For kit building I like a 5"-long, 46 teeth-per-inch blade, for other modeling tasks blades with fewer teeth per inch are better. These saws are so handy that it's worth owning two or even three of them.

❏ **Tweezers.** There may be an international standard for tweezer sizes, but I've never figured it out; several manufacturers label and number their tweezers differently. I prefer Inox No. 1, or tweezers labeled sizes MM and 3C. These are comfortable to hold and have strong, sharp points. It's worth having at least three pairs of your favorite size so you can always find at least one pair — this is particularly important if you have a layout which "swallows" your favorite tools.

❏ **Stainless-steel straightedges.** These are musts for straight, accurate cuts. Try to find the scale rule made by General that has O, S, HO, and N scales marked on it. I like to add a couple of thicknesses of masking tape on the back side of the

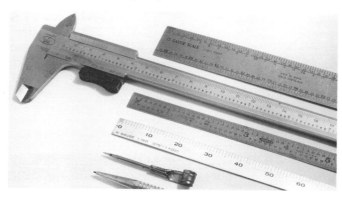

straightedge to lift it slightly off the work surface and to keep it from slipping while cutting. This is another tool that's worth having two of.

❏ **Jeweler's files.** Sometimes called needle files, a good beginner's set has six fine-cut files in various shapes. When you buy the files buy a brass bristled suede brush for cleaning them. Your files will work better if the teeth are clean. Just run the file brush over the file parallel with the teeth to remove material trapped between them.

❏ **Sanding blocks.** X-Acto sells a set of sanding blocks especially for model work, or you can spend a few minutes making your own. I have an assortment of sanding blocks made from 1" x 2", 2" x 2", and 1" x 3" pine scraps. Round the ends of the blocks so they

won't snag on your work.

Buy an assortment of sandpaper grades, say, from 80 grit to 220 grit, and install a different grade on each block. Wrap the sandpaper around the block and staple the ends to the top. To change the paper just pry out the staples.

For a really large sanding job glue a whole sheet of sandpaper to a flat board or a scrap piece of window glass. This is good for sanding the backs of the plaster castings used in a lot of craftsman kits.

❏ **Pliers and cutters.** Pliers are a must for bending wire, holding small parts while soldering, and for inserting pins. You'll need regular fine needle-nose pliers, subminiature long-nose pliers, and diagonal cutters. If you have a few extra dollars buy a pair of flush-cutting nippers also (the best ones are Lambert Rail Nippers from the hobby shop).

❏ **Miniature machinist's squares.** These are available in most hardware and hobby stores and from mail-order tool companies. The square is used for making cuts, marking and scribing, and is partic-

ularly good for keeping building sides square and true during assembly. Used with weights, a couple of squares form a great jig to hold parts perpendicular while the glue dries.

❏ **Soldering tools.** A 30-watt iron with a chisel tip is adequate for most kit-building work; you'll want at least a 100-watt soldering gun for layout wiring and other jobs where you need lots of heat.

I like 50-50 solid-core solder and a resin-based flux for most applications, but resin-core flux is handy for wiring, and acid flux works best for soldering sheet brass.

Alligator clips, other small metal clamps, or wads of wet tissue paper can be used as heat sinks when soldering small parts.

❏ **Scribers.** I use several scribers. The most useful was made from a school compass (for drawing circles). I snapped off the pointed leg, sharpened the point, and wrapped tape around the top to form a cushioned handle. This tool works well for marking wood, plastic, or plaster.

A commercial carbide-tipped scriber (check your hardware store) is handy for marking metal or glass.

❏ **Metal 90-degree triangle.** The simple metal triangle from a child's school pencil box is useful for squaring inside corners of structures and for laying out building sides and roofs. Because it's metal, you can also use it as a cutting guide.

❏ **Paint brushes.** Every modeler should own two types of paintbrushes — very expensive ones and very cheap ones. You'll need five or six top-quality brushes purchased at an art-supply store, and a couple of dozen cheap, throw-away ones.

Your selection of good brushes should include No.6 and No. 12 shovel-nosed sable brushes (sometimes called brights or filbert tips), as well as smaller No. 1 flat sable and Nos. 1, 6, and 12 round sable watercolor brushes. Take care of these as if your life depends on them, and they'll last a long, long time.

Cheap brushes are sold by the dozen in hardware, five-and-dime, and discount stores. These are useful for spreading white glue, applying plastic cement, staining stripwood, and particularly for spreading materials which require that you discard the brush afterward.

❏ **Pin vises.** You'll use a pin vise as a miniature hand drill, but it's also useful for holding small parts. Hobby shops and ship modeling catalogs sell them; it's worth owning three or four different sizes.

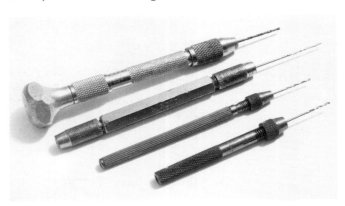

(By the way, the four-collet pin vise that X-Acto's been selling for the last 20 years isn't worth a plugged nickel).

A FEW ADVANCED TOOLS

You won't need these at first, but after you've used a few you'll wonder how you got along without them.

❏ **Dremel tools.** For starters, buy one of the top-of-the-line Moto-Tool kits with the built-in variable speed control. Eventually you'll need extra cutting burrs and a box of cut-off disks; ultimately it makes sense to have two motor tools at your bench — one with your favorite accessory permanently chucked in it, and one for everything else. Dremel's best accessory is their drill-press attachment; it takes a while to get used to if you've operated a real drill press, but once you do, it's really handy.

❏ **Paper cutter.** It may seem like a luxury, but a medium-size paper cutter is one of my most-used tools around the craftsman bench. It's fine for paper

and light cardboard, of course, but it also comes in handy for thin styrene sheet and corrugated aluminum siding.

❏ **Silver solder.** For extra-strong joints that will not come apart at the temperatures that melt regular solder, try Stay-Brite silver-bearing solder and flux. It's sold through specialty suppliers and discount tool catalogs. For heavy work you'll also need a small torch to melt this stuff.

❏ **Hot knives and wood-burning tools.** A hot knife is a great tool for cutting Styrofoam, sculpting and weathering wood, and selectively warping styrene parts. The most common version consists of a No. 11 X-Acto blade held in an adapted soldering iron or wood-burning iron handle.

I often use a hot knife to burn joints in the ends of milled wood clapboard siding. Don't overdo it or

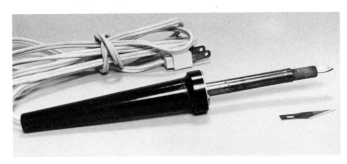

you'll make a caricature out of the siding. Follow up with a heated needle in a pin vise to make nail-hole detail.

Also useful is the wood-burning tool that comes in a kid's wood-burning set. Although you can't control the heat, you can alter the tip with a file for a better shape.

A top-of-the-line wood-burning tool, and a really handy item, is a lightweight, temperature-controlled

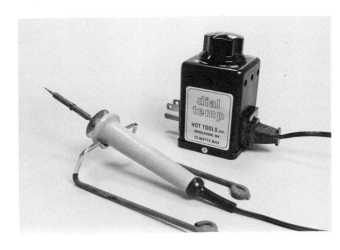

wood-burning iron called a "Hot Tool." This is used by the guys who carve duck decoys to add the very fine feather detail. It comes with wedge- and needle-point tips, and numerous other shapes are available.

THE BASIC ADHESIVES

The most useful adhesives for building craftsman kits are, in no particular order, white glue (Elmer's), ACC (Super Glue, Zap), Pliobond, 5-minute epoxy, and Testor's Cement for Plastics.

With liquid plastic cement there is always a danger of knocking the bottle over and ruining whatever project is on your workbench. The best way to keep the bottle from spilling is to drill a large hole in a scrap of 2" x 4" lumber and place the cement bottle in it. This stand holds the bottle while you apply cement — but you're on your own to remember to put that cap back on the bottle!

Pliobond is a heavy-duty rubber cement that will stick to nearly any clean surface. It can be used like regular glue, that is, you put a drop on each surface and hold them together until the glue dries, or it can be used as a contact cement. As a contact cement the Pliobond is brushed onto both flat surfaces and allowed to dry until slightly tacky. The parts are placed together in alignment (you only get one shot at this because once the parts touch you can't get them apart without destroying them), then weighted until the joint cures.

Pliobond can be thinned for easier application or to keep it from thickening. Use any solvent-type plastic cement (test it first by mixing a small amount in a bottle cap) or MEK (Methyl Ethyl Ketone). Add a few drops and stir well. Work in a well-ventilated area.

Epoxy will stick to most clean surfaces. I like 5-

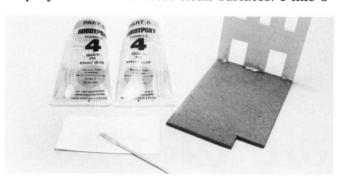

minute epoxies because they set rapidly. They are sold in most hardware and craft shops. The package consists of two tubes, resin and hardener, that are mixed together in equal portions. Mix them on a 3 x 5 card with a round toothpick. and mix only what you need — epoxy is expensive, but a little goes a long way.

USEFUL LOW-TECH WORKBENCH ITEMS

Go on a special Saturday-morning shopping trip and pick up some unusual items for your shop. You won't find many of them at the hobby shop. Buy a box each of the following: flat toothpicks, round toothpicks, Popsicle sticks, and tongue depressors. These are useful for spreading glue and mixing paint or glue.

While you're shopping, pick up 3 x 5 index cards, waxed paper, emery boards, masking tape, Scotch Magic tape (both kinds, standard and removeable), and denatured alcohol (a great thinner for shoe dye, and an excellent cleaner for plastic and metal parts before painting). Also you'll need some household items: Joy or other liquid dishwashing detergent; a cheap plastic mixing bowl; a rubber spatula or large spoon; teaspoon, tablespoon, and one-cup kitchen measures; paper cups; and several pump-type spray bottles, the kind used for misting plants.

GRAPH PAPER

Available in stationery stores, graph paper with

1/4" rulings makes excellent templates for building trestle bents, loading platforms, and anything else that has to be square or consists of regularly spaced parts.

Cover the graph paper with a piece of clear plastic to protect it from glue or place it under the sheet of glass on your workbench.

TRY A SHOT GLASS FOR YOUR GLUE!

Yes! The same glass the movie cowboys used when they bellied up to the bar and asked for a shot of Old Red-Eye can be used for dispensing glue. The best way to apply glue is to decant a small puddle onto a disposable surface, then dip into it with a toothpick or wire to carry the glue to the model. You probably already know this, and you've probably already dipped an elbow or the heel of your hand into the puddle of glue on your workbench, just like me.

Try this: Buy a couple of the cheapest, heaviest shot glasses you can find, preferably at a rummage sale. Wash one, then place it upside down on your bench. Most shot glasses have a depression or recess on the bottom, and this is the place to decant your glue.

Because the shot glass stands about 2-1/2" tall, you'll have a much harder time dipping parts of your anatomy into it. You'll also find that, right side up, the glass makes a great container for mixing small quantities of touch-up paint, for holding tiny parts, and for similar tasks. Really heavy shot glasses even make good weights.

Clean accumulated glue off the bottom of the glass

now and then with an old razor blade; for super glue you may need to follow up with a liberal application of acetone. ✿

Where to find the products

A-West Weather-it
Box 1144
Woodstock, GA 30188

Blue Ribbon Models
P.O. Box 333
Swampscott, MA 01907

Campbell Scale Models
P.O. Box 5307
Durango, CO 81301-6815

Dyna-Model Products Co.
Box 624
Sangerville, ME 04479

Evergreen Scale Models
12808 N.E. 125th Way
Kirkland, WA 98034

Fine Scale Miniatures
49 Main St.
Peabody, MA 01970

Floquil-Polly S Color Corp.
Route 30 N.
Amsterdam, NY 12010

Grandt Line Products
1040B Shary Ct.
Concord, CA 94518

M. Grumbacher, Inc.
460 West 34th St.
New York, NY 10001

Highball Ballast
P.O. Box 43633
Cincinnati, OH 45243

John's Lab
4915 Dean St.
Woodstock, IL 60098

Micro-Mark Model Tools
340-680 Snyder Ave.
Berkeley Heights, NJ 07922

MODEL RAILROADER
Kalmbach Publishing Co.
21027 Crossroads Circle
P.O. Box 1612
Waukesha, WI 53187

Northeastern Scale Models
99 Cross Street
P.O. Box 425
Methuen, MA 01844

Plastruct
1020 South Wallace Place
City of Industry, CA 91748

Railroad Model Craftsman
Carstens Publications, Inc.
P.O. Box 700
Newton, NJ 07860

Tamiya Paint
Model Rectifier Corp.
2500 Woodridge Ave.
Edison, NJ 08817

Vintage Reproductions
2606 Flintridge Drive
Colorado Springs, CO 80918

Wm. K. Walthers, Inc.
5601 W. Florist Ave.
Milwaukee, WI 53218

Campbell's HO structure kits come with some of the best instructions in the hobby, but you can still improve the kits by using them thoughtfully.

2
Tricks with kit instructions

BELIEVE IT OR NOT, most of the problems modelers have when building craftsman-type kits occur because they did NOT read and try to understand the instructions. So ...

READ THE INSTRUCTIONS — FIRST!

This is not a tip at all, just common sense. Don't be in a rush to start building. As builder, the most important consideration you have is "Do I understand the instruction sequence, and do I know where every part will go?"

Many well-planned kits have poor instructions, so it makes a lot of sense to read the instructions with all the materials and parts spread out on your workbench. Examine every part while you read the assembly sequence so you'll know where everything will go during the construction process. If you still don't understand them, read the instructions again!

IRONING THE INSTRUCTIONS

Yup, **iron** the instructions to get them flat! You'll be surprised how much help this is, particularly when the instructions include scale plans and templates — and most do.

Set the iron on steam, work carefully, and give each sheet a good flattening.

PROTECTING THE INSTRUCTIONS

In the process of building a kit we usually mess up the templates and scale drawings with glue, cut marks, and dripped paint. Sometimes the templates get to be unuseable before we're finished using them, and that's bad news. To protect the drawings purchase a large sheet of thin, clear, acetate to lay over the templates. Cut a piece to just cover the templates, tape it in place, and throw it away after the project is complete.

KEEPING YOUR PLACE

Most craftsman kits have extensive instructions, and keeping your place can be a chore. Here's a simple procedure that's worth making your standard:

❑ As you complete each step, draw a large check mark next to it.

❑ If you skip a step or a part of a step, draw a small square box (❑) next to it, indicating that there's something you've got to come back to.

❑ If you complete a portion of a step, but not the whole step, draw a line through the parts completed, but draw an open box (❑) to indicate that something's been skipped.

❑ As you complete a page or major portion of the instructions, draw a vertical line down the margin of the page to indicate that there's nothing left to do.

COPYING INSTRUCTION TEMPLATES

One way to speed up the construction of a project that requires repeated subassemblies of the same part is to photocopy the templates. That way, if you have to make something like trestle bents, you can be building several of the same thing at once, instead of wasting time waiting for the glue to dry on the first one.

CUTTING UP THE INSTRUCTIONS

The instruction sheets that come in craftsman kits belong to the purchaser, but I frequently ham-string myself by treating them as if they still belong to the manufacturer! Don't be afraid to cut up the instructions so you can use the plans as full-size templates for cutting window openings, etc. Also, when the instructions are printed on both sides, you can often save yourself a lot of page-turning if you simply photocopy one side.

FIND A PHOTO

One weakness of some craftsman kits is not providing photos of the completed model in the instructions. When you run up against one of these kits, find any photo you can of the model. The first place to look is in the manufacturer's ads; the second is in model magazine reviews. In the odd case you may even be able to find a photo of a built-up model on someone's layout in one of the magazines.

Unless the kit is awfully simple, finding a photo is always worth the search.

WORKING WITH SUBASSEMBLIES

With most kits you should follow the assembly sequence as the manufacturer has written it. The chief exception is to look for steps that can be performed out of sequence to make subassemblies — big sections of the model that can be built, detailed, then joined together to make the whole structure.

Why? Well, the main reason is that you always

want to handle the completed, or substantially completed, model as little as possible. If you drop your models (I do, a lot), this means what you drop is smaller, lighter, and (hopefully) the damage will be less.

The logical subassemblies for most wood structure kits are the individual walls. These can be built up, weathered, and windows and details installed while flat on the workbench, then assembled and touched up late in the construction sequence.

WORK ON WALLS FLAT

Particularly on fairly ornate buildings, it's always

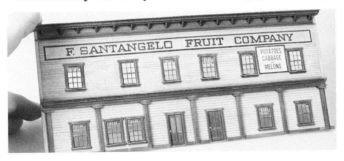

best to complete as much work as you can, up to and occasionally including the corner trim, while the walls are flat on the workbench. This is particularly important when the walls require a lot of touch-up painting or include such fragile features as decal signs.

ONLY ONE SIDE

When building a kit structure that will only be seen from one side on your layout, think about moving one or two windows or doors from the unseen side to the visible portions. You may be able to make the building different from all the others built from that kit — and more interesting.

USE YOUR IMAGINATION!

Before you start construction of a kit think about where the model will fit on your layout and how the total scene will look.

After looking at the layout you may decide to build the structure other that the way it's shown in the instruction sheet.

ASSEMBLING STRUCTURE WALLS

Here's where a sheet of glass, weights, and a couple of draftsman's or machinist's squares come in handy. I usually start by gluing one side and one end together, then do the same for the other side and end. When the first two joints set, glue the two L-shaped pieces together to form the basic building shell.

When something isn't quite straight, square, or perpendicular, split the difference among two or more joints. Remember, real buildings aren't perfect, either.

With the shell glued together, set it up on the glass sheet and weight it down with Popsicle sticks and weights so it dries flat and even on the bottom. ✪

Fine Scale Miniatures' HO rock crusher, issued several years ago, is a typical wood kit.

3
Working with wood and paper

DON'T LET THE TALK of high-tech modeling techniques scare you — wood and paper have been around for a long, long time, and they'll be around for many years to come. Best of all, wood and paper are among the most versatile and most enjoyable materials we can work with.

USE LOTS OF BRACING

One of the most discouraging things that can happen with a wood kit or a wood-and-card kit is to have it warp, either during construction or months later. The solution is to stock up on 3/16" square or even 1/4" square basswood, and add bracing inside the building walls. If you're not quite sure how

much bracing you need, think of the way a house is built with studs at regular intervals.

You won't need as much bracing as a carpenter puts in a house, but when in doubt, over brace!

YOUR OWN COLOR CODING

Occasionally you'll find a "stick kit" — one with lots of stripwood and lots of different sizes — where the wood isn't sorted or color coded. It's usually worthwhile (just to save time) to sort the wood and assign your own color code. That way, you won't spend a lot of time rummaging around for the right sizes as the instructions call them out. An assortment of fine-point watercolor markers (like Flair pens) does a neat job of the coding, and means you won't have to open jars of paint.

DISTRESSING WOOD

Among the many great tools for distressing wood are (from left to right) a Brookstone stainless-steel

scrubbing brush, a brass-bristled suede brush, a whitewall tire brush, a file card, and various small wire cleaning brushes. All are used by drawing the brush over the wood surface in the direction of the grain until the surface shows the desired amount of weathering.

A SPECIAL TOOL FOR SIDING BOARD ENDS

For adding board-end detail to wood siding, grind a hobby knife blade end down to the exact visible

width of one board, then sharpen. Simply by pushing this into the siding perpendicular to the surface you'll make perfect butt joints, with no danger of marring adjacent boards and spoiling the illusion.

ROLL SHINGLE TIPS

A few minutes spent randomly lifting and poking up the edges of Campbell or other roll-type shingles makes a world of difference in the appearance of the

finished model. It adds relief to what otherwise might be a rather plain roof. To further bring out the shingle detail the wall and roof can be stained, then dry-brushed to achieve a light-and-shadow effect.

Remember that shingled walls weather differently than shingled roofs. Wall colors will be brighter than the roof because the roof is exposed to the direct rays of the sun, which bleach it.

FINISHING THE SHINGLE JOB

Gummed kraft-paper wrapping tape, (the same stuff that Campbell shingles are made from), makes it easy to model cap and valley shingles.

Fold the paper and cut on either side of the fold to get the width you want the shingles to be. Then cut the folded strip into many V-shaped pieces. These are moistened and positioned with tweezers.

It's a little more work than the kit usually calls for, but the results are neater, more convincing and realistic.

WINDOWS THAT DON'T FIT

I once built a kit — no names mentioned — where the window castings fit inside (instead of over) the openings in the walls. The width of the window openings was fine — the castings had a nice, tight fit — but the castings were too short, by about 2 scale inches in HO.

The solution was to add pre-painted strips of 1/32" square stripwood across the top of each window casting. I did it to each one, and after a few months even I forgot the deception!

STRIPWOOD IN CAMPBELL KITS

Not all the instructions mention it, but most of the stripwood parts in Campbell structure kits can be identified by their length — the instructions call out the parts and tell how long they should be. It's a lot easier to measure the length of the stripwood than the tiny cross sections!

MODIFY THOSE EMERY BOARDS!

Emery boards are great for sanding small wood parts, and they work even better when you cut them up to fit the job at hand. Slice them in half, trim them to odd shapes, and throw them away when you're done. After all, the ladies use them only a few times before discarding them, and the new ones work a lot better than the worn-out kind.

PHONY WAINSCOTING

An old prototype trick is a good way to make a plain kit structure more interesting. Add a "phony wainscoting" stripe around the bottom edge of the

building. Start by painting the model in its basic wall color, then mask everything but a stripe around the bottom of the building that extends up to the bottom of the window trim.

Airbrush this stripe a contrasting color — usually darker — and spray from the taped area toward the bottom of the building to help keep the paint from getting under the tape.

YOU DON'T DO WINDOWS — UNTIL LATER

As mentioned in other tips, I like to build the walls of my structures as flat sub-assemblies. These are painted, weathered, and detailed before being assembled into the finished structure. The very last step in building the walls is the installation of the clear window material.

Windows installed last stay clear and shiny because none of the painting or weathering operations can mar the shininess of the glass. If you get a little glue on the glass, allow it to dry and pick it off with the tip of your X-Acto knife.

Reflection, not clearness, is what clean glazing gives you from most viewing angles, and reflection is what adds realism to your finished model.

REMOVING GLUE FROM BUILDING SIDING

Ever had the problem of white glue residue on wood walls built using board-by-board construction? Here's an easy way around it.

A steel wire brush in a motor tool makes quick work of whizzing away the glue, and works so well

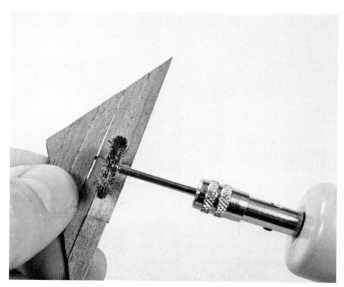

that it can zip away bits of the instruction sheet at the same time. This technique works so well that I no longer cover the instructions with waxed paper for board-by-board construction. Instead, I just glue the boards to the instructions with tiny dabs of white or yellow glue, then remove them later with the wire brush.

The ultimate application of this technique is to have a separate, battery-powered motor tool on your workbench just for removing glue. These tools cost about twenty bucks, and although the battery-powered tools are underpowered for most tasks, they're perfect for this one.

PILINGS AND HEAVY TIMBERS

A lot of the big round timbers I use for bridges, dams and pilings on my model railroads are built from balsa sticks. Start by buying 18" long by 1/2" square balsa strips from the hobby shop and round

the corners off with knives and heavy sandpaper.

Next, the pilings are cut to length and scraped with a wood rasp to produce a heavy wood grain. The grain is smoothed with sandpaper, stained a dull gray or brown color, and highlighted with white dry-brushing.

Steel bands to keep pilings from splitting can be made from strips of one-ply Strathmore painted rusty black and glued around the top.

EXTRA DETAIL FOR CLAPBOARD SIDING

To detail wood siding walls, I use a technique that provides a lot of realism for relatively little effort. Before painting, go over the siding with an X-Acto knife, cutting in clapboard joints, splitting out boards, and adding other imperfections at random. Then make a miniature awl by mounting a needle in

a pin vise and use this to punch nail holes at likely spots.

What you wind up with is a caricature of detail (since most of the cuts and holes have to be oversize to show up), but the effect gives the model a subtle, weathered look that can is difficult to obtain almost any other way.

BOOM TOWN PAINTING

Boom towns (particularly in our Wild West), contained buildings which were all front and no back. The side of the building that met the public eye was brightly painted with large, gaily colored signs, but the back walls were the dingy, weathered silver of unpainted wood.

WHEN PARTS WON'T FIT

Don't lose a lot of sleep over parts that won't fit. Sanding and shimming — especially shimming with very thin stripwood — works fine, and the corrections are usually invisible, even in close-up photos.

SANDING, NOT CUTTING, PARTS TO SIZE

When a stripwood part has to fit exactly, don't try to cut it to the right length; instead, cut it a hair (about 1/64") oversize and sand it to fit, trial-fitting frequently.

When one piece of stripwood overhangs another, cut it oversize, cement in place, and sand flush with the overlapped piece after the glue has dried.

PHOTO MOUNTING BOARD FOR HOLDING SCRIBED SIDING

Here's the problem: You want to build a sprawling

board station platform to fit between existing tracks and scenery, and you're going to build it with scribed basswood siding. There's not enough clearance to brace the bottom surface of the platform to keep it from warping. You cut the siding to fit between the tracks, but you still can't figure out how to hold it in correct alignment and keep it flat during the painting, weathering, and refitting.

A solution I stumbled upon was to use a stiff, self-adhesive, pressure-sensitive, photo mounting board available from a camera store. I cut a sheet of this material to fit the irregular platform area, slightly undersize, then pressed it into place. I then peeled off the protective paper and applied the sections of scribed wood to the pressure-sensitive surface.

It was then a simple matter to pry up the mounting board with the platform sheathing in place, take it to the workbench, and add thin square basswood bracing to the back. That done, I painted and weathered the assembly, let it dry, and reinstalled it on the layout.

I had to cut channels in the scenery to clear the bracing pieces (I used a steel cutter in a Dremel tool). Then I applied lots of white glue to the bracing and the back of the mounting board, worked it into place, set weights on it, and let it dry overnight.

STOPPING WOOD WALLS FROM SPLITTING

Back wood walls with masking tape while you cut out window and door openings. The tape keeps the wood from splitting as you make the break-through

cuts, especially where there is only a narrow band of wood between two openings.

After all the openings are cut and sanded to fit the castings, carefully remove the tape — or leave it in place if it won't interfere with gluing later.

MODIFYING WOOD KITS

The idea of buying a standard kit and bashing it into something more appropriate for your railroad just doesn't occur to most of us. But you can modify wood kits — it's not illegal — and the results can be

distinctive buildings for your layout. Think about changing roofing material, repositioning chimneys and pipes, doors, windows, and adding features.

This sort of kitbashing is especially good for making a building fit into an unlikely area. Some modelers even shop flea markets and try to find several of the same kits with a few parts missing.

INSTALLING CASTINGS IN WALLS

Super glue is great for cementing door and window castings into their openings. Align the casting and touch a drop of the glue to the back of the joint — it will distribute itself by capillary action.

If a little adhesive works its way onto the outside of the wall, soak it up with a twirl of rolled-up paper towel and touch up the glossy spot later with a brush and Testor's Dullcote.

REINFORCEMENTS

A lot of kits have you butt-glue two or three sections of siding together, which gives you a thin, weak joint.

Where they won't be seen, such as on the backs of walls or the bottom of a board platform, add strips of Scotch No. 810 Magic Tape as simple reinforcements.

SUBSTITUTING FOR INADEQUATE KIT PARTS

Don't hesitate to substitute for inadequate kit parts. Doing so can save you a lot of time and yield better results. I remember one Muir Models kit where Grandt windows were provided for everything but a complex bay-window assembly.

By purchasing a package of Grandt castings suitable for the bay I saved myself at least two evenings of construction time — and came up with a more pleasing model.

So don't think you're stuck with what comes in the box!

ALTERING CAMPBELL PLASTIC WINDOW AND DOOR CASTINGS

Something about Campbell window and door castings has always bothered me: those little "ears" that project on either side of the top trim board. I've seen relatively few real buildings with millwork like this, so I routinely trim the top boards flush with the

sides to make the windows and doors more to my liking.

BUILDING WITH PAPER

The use of Strathmore artist's paper for building models was popularized in the mid-fifties by Jack Work and Bill Clouser in MODEL RAILROADER

magazine. Their techniques for constructing complete structures using nothing but Strathmore board, glue, and paint were revolutionary. The resulting models were realistic — and very inexpensive to build.

Many modelers followed their examples, and many interesting and useful techniques were developed. Some modelers combined the Strathmore techniques with printed and textured building papers. These construction papers duplicate the texture of brick, stone, and tile.

Building papers have always been more popular in Europe than in the U.S. and are sold by several companies. The most complete source is the Wm. K. Walthers catalog (see the address list at the back of this book for more information).

USING BUILDING PAPERS

A good rule to follow is to use building papers on structures that will be placed in the background of your layout.

The construction sequence goes as follows:

❑ Glue the paper to a stiff cardboard or wood backing with rubber cement or Scotch Spray-Ment.

❑ Cut out the walls and roof and all the window and door openings.

❑ Dull the colors with thinned paint washes, dirty thinner, pastels, or a light airbrush overspray. If the papers have a slight shine, give them a coat of Testor's Dullcote; after it dries dust the paper lightly with gray or brown pastel chalk to tone down the coloring.

❑ Assemble the building sides by adding the windows and doors and any other detail. Add the roof last.

PAPER RETAINING WALLS

Brick and stone papers make good retaining walls, especially if they'll be a few inches back from the front edge of the layout. Add a few homegrown vines or some lichen tufts around the edges and you'll be surprised how good they look.

STONE-PAPER FOUNDATIONS

A lot of kit manufacturers provide kits without any type of foundation. In most cases this is not prototypical. Simple but realistic foundations can be built from stripwood covered with stone or brick building paper.

TEXTURING PRINTED BUILDING PAPERS

The surface texture of printed building papers can be improved by rolling the sheet, using a hard rubber roller, over a sheet of coarse sandpaper.

Roll the surface evenly, embossing the sandpaper texture into the building paper. For a coarser surface use rougher sandpaper. This method does not emboss the individual bricks, stones, and slates, but it does impart a rough, uneven texture to the surface of the paper.

COLORING EMBOSSED BUILDING SHEETS

Many kits suggest mounting embossed texture materials, either plastic or paper, on the model before coloring it, but I suggest going just the other way: Color the entire sheet while it's flat on the bench, then cut the needed portions.

I've colored embossed-paper brick sheet by applying a very thin coat of red stamp-pad ink to the surface with a finger, leaving some of the white color of the mortar lines showing through.

The requirements for this technique are patience, a nearly dry application of color, and practice. A similar technique works with fieldstone and other textures, substituting colored pencils for the stamp-pad ink.

SCRIBING STRATHMORE BOARD

My favorite scribing tool for Strathmore is the pointed end of a grade-school compass which I've dulled and rounded just a bit with emery paper.

The trick in scribing Strathmore is to apply just

enough pressure at the proper angle to indent, but not tear, the surface. Work under good light so that you can see how deep the scribing is. If you bear down too hard you'll stretch the Strathmore, causing it to warp and buckle, then you'll need extra bracing.

TEXTURING STRATHMORE BOARD

Wood grain, knotholes, and split or broken wood can be simulated by working the surface of Strath-

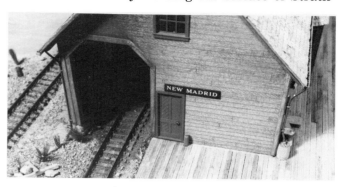

more board while it's still flat on the workbench, before assembly and staining. I use a fine needle to add wood grain to the scribed Strathmore. Push the needle point into the Strathmore to make knotholes, and use a sharp X-Acto knife to cut away jagged portions of boards to simulate cracking and splitting.

MARKING WINDOW AND DOOR LOCATIONS ON STRATHMORE BOARD

After you've finished laying out a building on Strathmore board and have scribed the wood siding and added the nail holes, it's time to mark the window and door locations.

I mark these locations with a very sharp pin or awl. Push the awl through each corner of every door and window location and at the building corners. The marking ensures that the door and window openings will not be covered up and lost during staining.

After painting, cut out each door and window opening with a very sharp X-Acto knife and a straightedge and scribe the corners for easy folding. Also, carve out some boards on the wall surface to show aging or wear.

USING CARDBOARD STRUCTURE BOOKS

Several companies offer cut-out or punch-out structure books in popular model railroad scales. These cardboard buildings make good stand-ins until more detailed buildings can be built. They can even serve as scale plans and templates for building detailed replicas. Eventually, when the cardboard buildings are replaced by something better, you can move the cardboard structure to the rear of the layout or salvage the printed signs and other parts.

These mock-ups are also handy for assessing the overall effect of groups of buildings in a town or industrial complex, but the best things about them are that they are easy to build, go together quickly, and are fun!

Dover Publications, 180 Varick St., New York, NY 10014, produces a series of HO scale printed build-

ings in book form. These full-colored, flat cardboard structures can be cut out, folded, glued together and set in place on the railroad. Straight from the book they look flat — like cardboard buildings — but with a little aging and weathering they can be real eye-catchers if used near the rear of your layout.

Most of the extra treatment can be performed before assembly, while the building is still flat. The first step is to visualize how the building would look under a light source and add shadows accordingly. Use soft lead pencils and draw the shadows, making them darker as they get closer to the eaves and other overhangs. Warped or protruding siding can be simulated by adding shadows under the boards that are warped. A selection of colored pencils will allow you to tint the shadows to reflect the siding or trim colors.

Next, weather the siding by fading and removing the paint (ink) using an ink eraser. Erase in the direction of the building's siding, using an erasing shield sold at drafting supply stores. The shield controls the erasure and masks the eraser from marring unwanted areas. Work on the building siding, trim, and roof to remove the paint unevenly, a little at a time, until you have the look you want. Using a soft lead pencil add board ends, cracks, and nail holes. With the erasing shield you can selectively lighten portions of the windows to simulate reflections. These lighter areas can be tinted with the colored pencils to show the reflection of the sky or of the surrounding scenery.

Last, before assembling the building, add three-dimensional details. These could include extra trim around the base, objects in the windows like fans or air conditioners, signs, skylights, glazing in the cut-out windows, even interior details, balconies, railings and steps.

WHEN THE WOOD ISN'T "FUZZ FREE"

Some kits come with clean, accurately sawn and milled wood parts, some don't. Here are three ways

to deal with the problem of fuzzy wood.

First, sand all stripwood. Do this by drawing each strip, with the grain, across a sanding block covered with 150-grit sandpaper — eight times! Yup, eight times — once for each side, and once for each corner. The corner sanding, particularly, eliminates the unattractive "raw" look you'll see in some wood models.

Second, go over fuzzy sheetwood with extra-fine steel wool to remove the worst fuzz, then follow up with a brass-bristled suede brush to remove the rest and moderately distress the wood. Again, work with the grain.

Another way to deal with fuzzy sheetwood is to sweep the flame of a propane torch across the surface. Obviously, a light touch is called for, but this technique will work. The heat will drive the moisture out of the wood, causing it to curl toward the treated side, but you can either give it a couple of days to straighten out or sweep the back of the wood with the flame to equalize the warping. Oh yes — don't try this with stripwood: It disappears! ✺

This string of downtown building flats was kitbashed from leftovers from other plastic structure projects.

4
Plastic structure tricks and kitbashing

MORE AND MORE, the modeling world doesn't break down neatly into two simple categories of "craftsman" and "plastic." Instead, there now exists a varied category of what might be called "plastic craftsman" kits, often made of modern polymer casting resins and produced from scratchbuilt originals. These new kits, plus the traditional injection-molded plastic structure models, offer excellent grist for building top-notch structures for your layout — structures that can be made indistirguishable from your best craftsman-kit and scratchbuilt structures.

Here's a handful of tips for making plastic look better than you thought it could!

DISTRESSING PLASTIC SIDING

A fast way to add wood grain texture to plain styrene sheathing is with coarse sandpaper (40- or 60-grit), rubbed in the direction of the wood grain, followed by a good smoothing with a soft brass bris-

tled suede brush, again stroking in the same direction as the wood grain.

The sandpaper gives the plastic a deep, rough, texture and the suede brush smooths away surface roughness and "fuzzies" while keeping the grain effect.

IMPROVING PLASTIC STRIP STOCK

To eliminate the raw, overly precise look of Evergreen plastic strips, sand, wire brush, and use steel wool to remove the crisp edges.

DULLING THE PLASTIC SHINE

If you don't do anything else to a kit-built plastic structure, at least spray on a good coat of Testor's

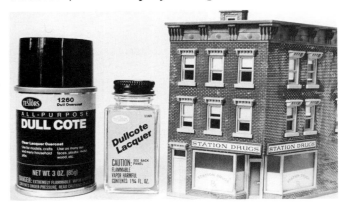

Dullcote after assembly, but before installing the clear window glazing. After gluing in the windows, dust the whole building with finely ground, earth-colored pastel chalks to further deaden the Dullcote's matte finish.

For more weathering techniques see Chapter 9.

SAWING POLYESTER BUILDINGS

To cleanly saw Magnuson (now Walthers') polyester building walls into sections, use a table saw with a plywood blade installed backwards, that is,

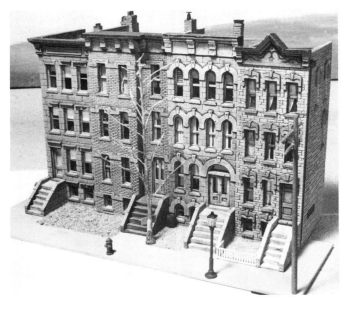

with the teeth facing away from the normal direction of rotation.

Cutting the walls with the blade set this way yields a crisp, clean edge that needs no further preparation before assembly. Just be sure you reori-

ent the blade before you use it again for sawing wood!

FLATTENING POLYESTER WALLS

Due to the way they're made, the Magnuson polyester building kits occasionally come out of the box with bowed wall castings. They can be flattened by placing them on a slab of 3/4" plywood or particle board, heating your kitchen oven to 150 degrees F., and putting the walls in the oven for 30 to 60 minutes until they "relax" and flatten out. Allow the walls to cool slowly, and they'll stay flat. Use a thermometer to check the oven temperature, because most oven thermostats are wildly inaccurate.

QUICK WOOD-CORE STYRENE BUILDINGS

Small styrene buildings can be built around a solid wood block. The advantages to doing so are rigidity, speed, and ease of construction. The block can be made on a table saw set up to the inside dimensions of the building.

Cut window and door openings in the styrene siding before gluing it to the wood block. Door and window castings must be pre-glazed with frosted acetate before they are glued into the walls. Glue the completed walls around the block and add corner trim.

Roofs can be formed from shingle-textured styrene or from molded roof parts stolen from a kit.

MAKING ODD-SIZED CHIMNEYS

It's easy to model odd-sized chimneys. Simply build

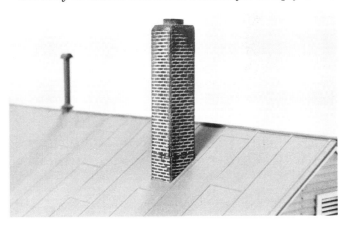

up layers of styrene brick sheet around a plastic or wood core.

MAKING THE MOST OF COMMERCIAL MILLWORK PARTS

One of the best ways to plan your next scratch-built structure is to design it around existing, commercially available window and door castings. Sometimes this means altering the look of the building slightly, especially if you are working from a specific prototype. However, the savings in time is great, and construction is a whole lot easier than it would be if you scratchbuilt the windows and doors.

THIN-MULLIONED WINDOWS

To model the thin-mullioned windows found on older stations, turn Grandt Line windows upside down, trim them to the proper height and width, reassemble, and insert them into the walls from the inside. Then add trim to the outside surface of the wall.

PREPARING CASTINGS FOR PAINTING

Denatured alcohol (shellac thinner) is a good pre-painting wash for castings because it removes oil, grease, and silicone mold-release lubricants, dries quickly, and leaves no residue. I give plastic or metal castings a 10-15 minute soaking in a wide-mouth jar of denatured alcohol. Remove the parts from the alcohol with tweezers, then spread them out on paper towels to air-dry.

Don't handle the parts with your fingers until after they have been installed and painted, and the paint has had plenty of time to dry.

After every three or four kits I pour the alcohol down the drain and replace it with fresh. If you build lots of kits, denatured alcohol comes pretty cheap by the gallon.

Large doses of denatured alcohol fumes aren't good for you, so work only in a well-ventilated area.

EUROPEAN KITS FOR AMERICAN BUILDINGS

The prototypes of a lot of HO plastic building kits are rather obviously European, but a long, hard look beneath some of the "facial" details reveals buildings that, given some careful attention to painting and weathering and a few minor changes, can easily fill the bill for buildings on U.S. and Canadian pikes. This is especially true of masonry structures, where the basic construction was the same on both sides of the "pond."

BASIC PLASTIC KIT ASSEMBLY

It seems pretty obvious, but when the molded-in pins, tabs, and alignment lugs in a plastic kit prevent proper alignment, the best thing to do is eliminate them.

Once you cut the pins off, assembly becomes a matter of aligning parts by hand and eye — just as you would a craftsman kit!

A NEW LOOK FOR OLD KITS

One way to radically alter and improve the look of some of the old-standby plastic kits is to replace the molded-in windows and doors with separate castings. My Revell HO farmhouse is a good example: I back-dated it by replacing the wide, large-pane windows with narrow, multiple-pane Grandt-Line cast-

ings. This also eliminates the need for the painted-acetate window inserts in the kit, and vastly improves the model. Plus, it's fun to have one of these 30-year-old kits, much improved, on my layout.

DON'T FORGET THOSE LEFTOVERS!

Some of my favorite buildings have been made from the bits and pieces left over from more-exten-

sive plastic kitbashing projects. Here's one of them: A homely little brick office building made from odds and ends of Revell HO enginehouse walls. ✪

5
Tips for using metal castings

ONE OF THE WAYS that craftsman kits differ from other types of models is that they often include large numbers of highly detailed metal castings. If you've never worked with such castings, preparing them, cementing them to the other materials in the kit, and, above all, painting them effectively can be a challenge. Here are tips for mastering castings.

SANDING METAL CASTINGS

A sanding block, just like the one you use for shaping and fitting plastic, wood, and plaster walls, works great on soft-metal castings. Rub the castings over the block to square them and to remove excess edge flash. Use the tip of an X-Acto knife to remove interior flash.

VINEGAR TO CLEAN AND ETCH CASTINGS

Some white metal and brass castings do not hold paint well because the surface is smooth or contaminated with mold-release agents. A quick way to prepare the casting surface and clean it at the same time is to soak the castings in full-strength white household vinegar.

Fifteen minutes is long enough to etch the surface slightly before painting (any longer could harm the castings). Wash the castings with tap water and allow them to air-dry overnight before painting.

DRILLING IN SOFT METAL

If you have to drill a lot of holes in soft metal, such as the white-metal castings found in craftsman kits, you'll need a cake of beeswax (from a sewing goods

store). Lubricate your drill by running it into the beeswax cake before starting each hole. Back the

drill off every now and then to clear away the metal chips and beeswax residue.

For deep holes, re-lubricate the drill tip every time you remove the bit to clear the hole.

Where the hole size is important, drill first with the next-smaller-size numbered drill, then ream the hole to size with the required size.

CLEANING BRASS

The best way to clean brass parts before painting is with tooth powder applied with an old toothbrush. The toothbrush bristles get into all the nooks and crannies and the powder removes all the leftover soldering flux and finger oils. Use the toothbrush

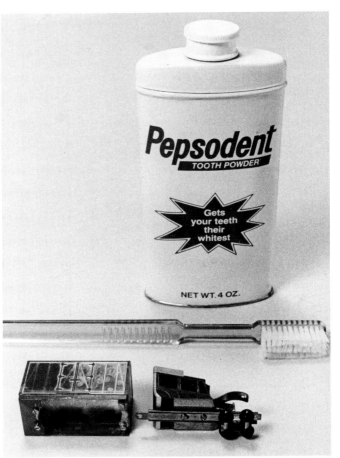

just as you would if you were brushing your teeth only be gentle — you don't want to damage any of your hard work.

Making metal castings match weathered wood, as on this Fine Scale Miniatures kit, is a real modeling challenge.

Wash the brass parts with soap and warm water, allow to air-dry, then handle the parts only with tweezers until they're painted. If you want to continue the cleaning process further, add denatured alcohol to your ultrasonic cleaner and run the cleaner for about ten minutes.

WARPED METAL CASTINGS

Warped white-metal castings, especially doors and windows, can be straightened or flattened by gently pressing them against a sheet of glass.

CEMENTING BIG METAL CASTINGS

The instructions in most metal kits recommend using ACC (Super-Glue, Zap, etc.) to cement the parts, but I find ACC is not strong enough for a heavy kit or one that takes a lot of handling to build.

Instead, use a two-part, 5-minute epoxy for all the basic building assemblies and use ACC only for the details. This will slow construction a little, but time will be saved because you will not have to re-glue any of the major joints later on.

MATCHING CAST DOORS AND WINDOWS

One of the hardest things to do is make cast metal (or plastic) doors and windows match weathered wood wall sections. This is particularly difficult in some of the Fine Scale Miniatures kits, where the wood can be stained to a beautiful weathered finish, and you have to somehow make the castings match or risk an unconvincing finished model.

"Clean" is the first watchword: Remove all traces of flash, mold parting lines, and sprue-attachment points from the castings with knife and files, then toss them all into a wide-mouth bottle of full-strength denatured alcohol for 10 to 30 minutes. Fish the parts out with tweezers — no fingers until they're painted — and drop them onto paper towels to dry.

When the parts have dried, spread them out on cardboard slabs covered with masking tape strips with the sticky side up. Usually, you only need to paint one side, but the masking tape allows positioning parts on edge so that you can paint both sides if necessary.

Now airbrush the parts with a mixture of 75 percent Floquil RR-84 Foundation, 20 percent Dio-Sol, and 5 percent Glaze. (These are the standard proportions of paint, Dio-Sol, and Glaze for airbrushing any Floquil color.) For plastic parts keep the airbrush far enough away that the paint is partly dry when it hits the surface.

Next, wait (this is the hard part). Let the Foundation coat dry for a week (10 days is better) before following up with Flo-Stains, paints, washes, or alcohol stains. Once thoroughly dry, the Foundation is impervious to solvents (even Dio-Sol). Its light, pinkish-buff color allows the castings to accept other coloring media in a manner very similar to unpainted wood; if you want to, you can match stained or painted wood exactly.

If you want to get the castings for a kit painted so they can dry but aren't sure what colors to use, spray them with Foundation, then put them aside. Later, it's a simple matter to add your final colors over the neutral Foundation base color during assembly. ✪

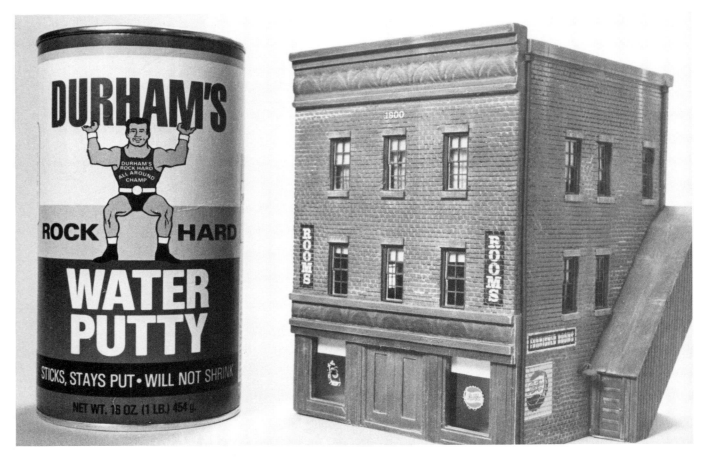

Durham's Water Putty is an excellent filler for the dental-stone castings used in plaster kits.

6
Techniques for plaster buildings

IT WAS OVER 15 YEARS AGO when the first cast-plaster building kits came along. These buildings are almost the exact opposite of mass-produced models. The wall sections are reproduced from hand-built masters and the kits are made in limited quantities. In effect, these kits give you a handmade product for your layout.

Many of the techniques in this chapter can be applied to coloring other scenery items, such as homemade cast-plaster retaining walls.

EXTRA CRACK FILLER FOR PLASTER KITS

It's easy to run out of the tiny supply of dental-stone powder supplied to fill in the corner gaps of plaster building kits. When you do, use Durham's Rock Hard Water Putty, available at most hardware stores. Durham's Water Putty (photo above) is virtually the same color as dental stone, has similar

working characteristics, and takes paint the same way.

PLASTER PARTS ARE THIRSTY!

Seal the walls of plaster buildings if you plan to paint them with anything but water-soluble paints. If you don't seal them and use thinner-based paints, keep in mind just how "thirsty" dry plaster is.

One good sealing material is Krylon No. 1303 Crystal Clear, which comes in an aerosol can (if you have trouble finding this material, try an art-supply store; Krylon No. 1311 works about the same). The Crystal Clear prevents paint from disappearing into the thirsty plaster and also makes hard and soft spots in the plaster accept coloring uniformly.

Because plaster is so very thirsty, when coloring plaster parts it's always best to err on the light side. Use thin washes and wait until the paint dries

before evaluating your results. Applying a wash that's too dark is murder, because to recover from it you must coat the plaster parts with a light-colored opaque paint, then try again.

STAINING PLASTER PARTS

One very controllable coloring approach is to use greatly thinned paint washes followed with a dusting of powdered pastel chalks. Spray a coat of clear flat finish such as Testor's Dullcote to seal the pastel against the plaster.

Always test your stain on the back of the cast-plaster pieces first, and if you have trouble controlling the intensity of the tint, try spraying the casting with water before coloring it. Remember, the plaster will always dry to a lighter shade than it appears during application.

BUILDING YOUR OWN MASONRY

Modeling realistic stonework can be a tiring and repetitive process. You can speed up wall building by carving a small, interlocking portion of the wall or

foundation, then making an RTV rubber mold of it. From this mold many castings can be made using molding plaster or Hydrocal. The resulting castings can be cut up and rearranged to form all sorts of rock work that looks nothing like the original.

MASONRY DIMENSIONS

The approximate size of regular clay bricks is 8" x 2 1/4" x 3 3/4". Bricks have roughly 1/4" to 1/2" of mortar around them.

Standard cement blocks measure about 8" x 15 3/4" x 7 3/4".

HOW TO MAKE A WALL MASTER

Glue about a dozen pieces of scale 18"-square by 36"-long stripwood to a piece of scrap plywood. Arrange the pieces so there is roughly 1/4" between strips. Build a dam of plywood or matte board around the strips and fill the cavity with Dow-Corning or General Electric RTV rubber. The stripwood pieces will become the patterns for the "stones" used to build your master wall.

The rubber will set in from 5 to 20 hours, depending on the brand and the amount of catalyst that you add. When it does, peel the mold away from the stripwood patterns.

Fill the mold with Durham's Water Putty to make plaster replicas of the stripwood pieces. Allow the Durham's to set overnight, then carefully pop the pieces from the mold.

Next, saw the strips into stone-sized pieces. Carve one face of each stone with the tip of an X-Acto knife until it looks like a hand-hewn stone. The best technique is to chip away the rock face so that each knife stroke pulls material away from the stone, leaving ragged plaster behind. Each rock you carve will become a master rock and will be used as a pattern for future walls, so any extra time spent at this stage will be worth it.

Stack and arrange the individual stones with white glue on another slab of plywood to make a section of masonry wall. Each wall section should be the same height as and be able to interlock with its neighbor. Assemble as many sections as needed.

Finally, make an RTV mold of each section, then cast finished wall sections in molding plaster, Hydrocal, or Durham's. The resulting castings can be mated, painted, and glued in place on your layout for retaining walls, or used to make building foundations or whole structure walls.

REWORKING DENTAL STONE

Dental stone in particular, and the plaster supplied with most kits in general, is easier to carve if you remoisten it with "wet" water (add a teaspoon of dishwashing detergent to a pint of water) first.

PAINTING PLASTER SMOKESTACKS

Seal the raw plaster with Floquil RR5 Glaze, Krylon No. 1303 Crystal Clear spray, or a sanding sealer, then apply gray paint to simulate the mortar color. When this has dried thoroughly — several days minimum — apply a brick red or buff color. Use light strokes and a daubing motion with a wide brush or a make a daubing pad from a piece of old T-shirt. The idea is to apply the color only to the faces of the brick, leaving the mortar color showing in the cracks.

Two other things to keep in mind when installing a big industrial smokestack: First, these stacks are heavy, and unless the structure you put under them is clearly capable of supporting them, they'll look silly. Second, the stack, particularly the top lip, should be dirty, with at least a suggestion of soot stains and streaks.

Lettering, such as a factory name or perhaps your railroad name or initials, always looks great on these stacks.

COLORING PLASTER WITH ACRYLICS

One way to color plaster walls — either from a kit or homemade — is to use techniques adapted from water-soluble scenery, and that means acrylic paints. Above all, coloring wall castings is not art — it's simply common sense combined with a little

research. I like colors lighter than the prototype, mainly because there's a lot less light shining on my layout than there is on the real thing.

Here's what you'll need:
- ❑ Joy or other liquid dishwashing detergent
- ❑ a pump-type spray bottle

- ❑ Polly S, flat household latex paint, acrylic artist's tube colors, or other acrylic colors
- ❑ black India ink
- ❑ paintbrushes
- ❑ shallow dishes for mixing colors
- ❑ a shot glass

I color wall castings just after they have set, while the plaster is still damp. Wet dry castings, such as those from a kit, by soaking them in water or by flooding them with water from the spray bottle.

Start by spraying the casting with a black wash made by mixing 1/2 teaspoon of India ink, 1 quart of water, and 4 drops of liquid dish detergent. Use plenty of the black wash, enough that the excess runs off. Then proceed with the coloring.

For variety in wall coloring, try these formulas:

Basic brick wall: Mix 2 teaspoons Polly S Boxcar Red, several drops Polly S Roof Brown, and 4 drops liquid detergent to 6 ounces water in a spray bottle. Add more water to weaken the intensity.

Concrete Retaining Wall: Mix a 1" squeeze of Medium Gray with 1/2" of Raw Sienna acrylic tube color or 2 teaspoons Polly S Reefer Gray and 1/2 teaspoon Polly S Earth and 4 drops liquid detergent to 8 ounces water in spray bottle.

Red Granite Wall: Add 1/2 teaspoon Polly S Rust to the basic brick wall color.

Always experiment with new colors on the back of a wall or a piece of scrap plaster, and always evaluate colors *after* the plaster has dried.

The next step is to paint some of the individual bricks or stones a slightly different color. In a shallow dish, mix several tablespoons of basic wall color. Open several bottles of Polly S colors that are darker than the stones in the wall and a bottle of Reefer White. Work under your normal railroad-room lights. Pick up a brush load of Polly S paint from one of the jars and mix it with some of the wall color. Dab this onto the surface of a few bricks or stones, then evaluate the color.

If it looks good, continue painting individual stones at random. Wash the brush in fresh water, then try another color. Paint some of the stones a lighter color by mixing Reefer White with the basic wall color. Continue until about half the wall has different-colored bricks or stones, then allow the paint to dry completely.

The last step at the workbench is to dry-brush the highlights onto the wall to emphasize surface detail.

The wall castings can now be assembled. Weather the walls with thin acrylic washes and powered pastel chalks exactly as you would any other structure (see Chapter 9).

EPOXY FOR PLASTER WALLS

Plaster walls are substantial pieces, and when it comes to assembling them into a basic structure shell, you should plan on using a strong adhesive.

Although it's expensive, my favorite glue for this application is a two-part, 5-minute epoxy. I make a

small base for the building from scrap Masonite, then assemble the walls to it and to each other with generous amounts of epoxy. In fact, anytime there's

a little epoxy left over after mixing, I lather it into a corner joint to form an extra-strong fillet.

QUICK AND "DIRTY" CONCRETE COLORING

I've had good luck coloring cast-plaster parts that represent concrete with dirty Floquil thinner. Use a large brush to flow it on, and work from top to bottom in a well-ventilated area.

My thinner is usually a little darker than neutral gray (a mixture of all colors) but yours will depend on what colors your last several projects were, and this imparts a subtle variety to concrete structures colored at different times.

Need to color concrete sections but you don't have any dirty thinner? Make your own by combining equal parts Dio-Sol and Floquil RR82 Concrete with a few drops of Grimy Black, Mud, and Earth from Floquil's Weathering Colors set.

COLORING PLASTER WITH WATERCOLORS

Tube-type watercolors (available in art and craft stores) work well for coloring plaster. These paints are semi-liquid, and you squeeze only what you need from the tube. Choose the heavy-pigment colors, not the translucent colors or the stains. Start with the following: Erulean Yellow, Cadmium Yellow, Rose Madder, Alizarin Crimson, Cerulean Blue, and Burnt Sienna.

These starter colors can be combined to make realistic brick, stone wall and concrete colors. Please, don't let the fancy names confuse you, what you're really selecting are basic reds, yellows, blues, and earth shades. These can be combined on the palette to make all the other colors you need. As an example, make green by mixing yellow and blue or combine Burnt Sienna and Cerulean Blue for a nice neutral earth color — then add a little yellow and it becomes a good simulation of weathered copper.

I mix watercolors on a grade-school watercolor palette (enameled tin with lots of small paint depressions), but any nonporous surface will do, even a sheet of waxed paper. Squeeze a little (1/8") of each color onto the palette, and have a shot glass of clean water handy along with several wide brushes and a sheet of folded paper towel.

First, wet the plaster walls by brushing on clean water. This renders the castings less thirsty and allows the water color to flow into all the nooks and crannies without being immediately sucked into the plaster.

Dip the brush in the water and pick up a little of the basic building color, swirl it around on the palette, and apply it to the walls. If you're working on a brick building you'll want the base color to be red or red-yellow. Try this: With the side of the building flat, flow on a brush load of Erulean Yellow followed by Rose Madder. Clean the brush and dab on a light wash of Cerulean Blue mixed with a little

Burnt Sienna. The blue and Sienna will start to neutralize everything that you've done, so be careful.

The colors will settle into different areas, depending on the wetness of the plaster. If you think one color is a little heavy, rinse the brush, wipe it on the swatch of paper towel, then dab away the color. Dip the brush in the clean water and brush away the color until it looks light enough, or blot away excess color with the paper-towel pad.

Positioning the wall section so that the bottom edge is higher than the top will let darker colors run onto the undersurfaces of the stones. This is an effective technique for "painting in" shadows. Use the same technique for getting darker color under sashes, lintels, and other projections.

Now use a damp swatch of paper towel — the same one used to blot the brush — to lightly drag across the top surfaces of the stones. This highlights the top surfaces of the stones by allowing the light-colored plaster to show through.

Painting models with watercolors, or any other type of paint, is not art, but common sense and practice. Mixing or changing colors is not mysterious: For instance, to de-yellow a color, use more blue. Scrub it on with a broad brush until you achieve results you like.

Use Ultramarine blue to add shadows under the roof overhang and below window sills. Be careful with this — the color is really strong, almost black, so use a lot of water.

Yellow and blue will make a moss green. Brush it on the base of walls to look like areas where dampness has discolored the stones. This light green will let ground scenic foam or other scenic material automatically blend into colors on the wall. Don't use so much so that the wall surface looks green, just a hint of color is enough.

Watercolors dry down lighter than they appear when wet, so you'll have to wait until the walls dry before you can evaluate the coloring. If you don't like the results you can always re-paint. One nice side-effect with watercolors is that you get a lot of subtle color variations without really trying.

Once you become comfortable with watercolors you can mix the paints right on the walls to come up with unique weathering effects.

YES YOU CAN!

Okay, you've just shelled out thirty or forty bucks for a craftsman-type plaster structure kit, and while looking over the instructions a wild thought enters your head — the thing might fit in even better on your layout if you modified it here and there!

Trouble is, what you've paid for is somebody else's scratchbuilt original, and you feel at least slightly

guilty about cutting it up and making it look like something else.

Dismiss those guilty pangs! It's your building, and you've got every good reason to alter it to your tastes. Better yet, just like any kind of kitbashing, changing the model to coincide with your druthers will make it distinctively yours, and means it won't look like every building made from the same kit. ✪

Pete Laier kitbashed this Campbell HO brewery. A lot of the work involved altering roof angles.

7
Roofing ideas

IF YOUR RAILROAD is below eye level (and most of ours are), roof details are perhaps the most important aspects of your structures. Your visitors (and you!) see the roofs first, and the details there will convey the feeling of a finished, highly detailed model — even if the buildings underneath the roof are simple.

Remember, the more detail the roof displays, the more highly detailed the whole structure — and your layout — seems.

EASY-TO-MAKE ROOF DETAILS

Roof details that are quick and easy include cast-plastic ladders, roof walks (cast ladder stock

dropped on its side and planked with stripwood), fire barrels, skylights, ventilators, roof-access doors,

flagpoles with guy wires, fancy chimneys, and vent and stove pipes.

CARDBOARD ROOF TEMPLATES

The best way to lay out a complicated roof on your scratchbuilt structure is to make disposable cardboard patterns, fitting them to the roof by trial and error.

Roughly cut pieces of cardboard or matte board are placed on the structure to form the roof. Build up the

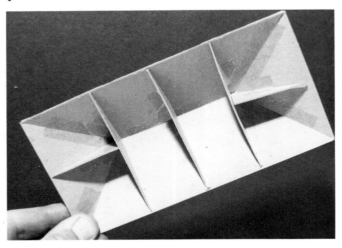

roof a piece at a time, cutting and trimming each section as you go. Hold all the sections in place with masking tape. The cardboard is positioned, trimmed and re-positioned until the fit and look is perfect. By this time the cardboard pattern should look like the completed roof; when it does, number the pieces with a marking pen so you can identify them later.

Remove the roof templates and carefully pull away the tape. Use these cardboard pieces as patterns to cut the final roof sections from textured material.

ROOF BRACING

If you're building a removable roof, brace it heavily.

I like to use 1/4"-square basswood or balsa around all the edges and 1/8"-thick triangular pieces inside the eaves.

TAR LINES

Around chimney bases and along the seams where two pieces of tarpaper meet the gaps are sealed with black roofing tar to keep water out. These tar lines are easy to model using either full-strength Mars

Black acrylic tube color or Polly S Gloss black, applied with a small brush. Don't worry about a shaky hand — the prototype is seldom neat!

CHIMNEY POTS

Chimney pots are not just for merry olde England, they were (and are) used in North America to sepa-

rate flues and enhance draft. On a model, chimney pots are great for making solid-topped chimneys look more "open."

Use brass tubing or ballpoint pen refills cut into sections about two scale feet high to represent the chimney pots. Glue them to the top of the chimney casting. As a finishing touch, don't forget to add a little "tar" around the joints.

TARPAPER ROOFING

For a simple tarpaper effect, spray cardboard roof halves with a spray adhesive such as Scotch Spray-Ment or 3M Super 77 Spray Adhesive. These spray adhesives are a sort of "tape in a can," but be sure to use them with plenty of ventilation.

For the tarpaper, cut strips of fine sandpaper or rough black construction paper with a paper cutter and position them over the spray-glued roof surface while the glue is still at least partially wet. The

strips will stay in place almost forever if you burnish them down lightly with your finger.

WORKING WITH CORRUGATED ALUMINUM SIDING

The thin corrugated aluminum supplied in Campbell and other craftsman kits presents unusual challenges, but it sure looks like the real thing if handled properly. When handling it during construction, work only on a clean, perfectly flat surface, because any irregularities will be duplicated in the thin

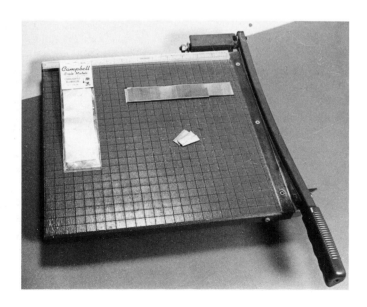

material. (A large pad of writing paper makes an excellent working surface.)

A paper cutter is a good tool for cutting numerous sections of corrugated siding or roofing. Bundle the large sheets in the kit so they won't slip when cut, and only work with four or five sheets at a time.

For cutting windows and door openings, use a sharp No. 11 X-Acto blade and don't hesitate to replace it. Blades dull quickly when you work with this material, and a dull blade is worse than no blade at all.

If you kink the aluminum during handling, try using your finger in a gentle stroking motion to smooth out the creases over a flat surface.

By far the best glue to use is a contact adhesive such as Pliobond, applied using the two-coat contact process (see Chapter 10).

PAINTING CORRUGATED ROOFING — TECHNIQUE 1

The rich, rust-brown color of corrugated roofing is hard to achieve, because not all weathering processes develop the same colors. There are as many ways

to deal with the thin, corrugated-aluminum siding material that comes in a lot of craftsman kits as there are modelers! The challenge in using any of these materials is twofold: First, we've got to find a way to make paint stick to the slippery corrugated stock; and second, we've got to color and weather it to look like either intact or rusted galvanized iron.

Here's a technique that's easy and works every time. First, assemble the portions of the building that will be covered with the corrugated material and apply the aluminum. Next, airbrush the completed building (or the wall and roof sections, if they aren't assembled yet) with a mixture of blue-gray Floquil. Make this by adding just a touch of a strong blue to Reefer Gray — the proportions aren't critical, and the idea is to pick up some of the blue of the sky that's reflected in galvanized metal.

Let the blue-gray dry thoroughly (up to a week is best), then airbrush over it with splotchy applications of Floquil Roof Brown, Boxcar Red, and Rust. Follow these colors with a generous coat of Testor's Dullcote, then let this second coating dry for a couple of days (another week, if you can stand it).

Finally, brush on powdered pastel chalks to blend the splotchy colors into the blue-gray base coat and one another. Build up the chalk powders heavily, and make them stronger than you think they should be. Then spray on another coat of Dullcote, sealing the chalk powders in place and moderating their vibrancy.

The result is a realistic rich-rust look, and you can keep building it up with successive coats of chalk powder and Dullcote.

PAINTING CORRUGATED ROOFING — TECHNIQUE 2

DANGER! Before we start, admit to yourself that this technique is DANGEROUS, period. It involves etching the aluminum with a highly corrosive chemical, and if you don't take the right precautions, you

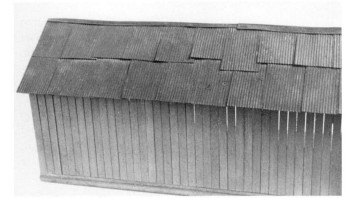

can hurt yourself — badly. But, like so many things in life, if you do take the right precautions, you'll not only be plenty safe, but you'll achieve astounding results.

Here's what you'll need:

❏ Archer Etchant from Radio Shack, or another printed-circuit-board etching solution. This is ferric chloride, and you should treat it like full-strength acid.

❏ Rubber gloves, the heavier the better.
❏ Large tweezers
❏ Safety glasses

❏ Two shallow, wide-mouth jars or glasses
❏ Paper towels

Start by cutting up all the corrugated material you plan to use into scale-size sheets. The kit should tell you what size to make them. If you have a paper cutter, it works well for the cutting.

Decant about an inch of the Archer Etchant into one of the jars, and put two or three inches of cold water in the other. Put on the gloves and safety glasses, and cover your working surface with a pad of old newspaper or a double thickness of paper towel.

Now drop the first corrugated aluminum section into the etchant. Poke it under with the tweezers. For what seems like a long time nothing will happen, but as soon as the section starts to fizz and foam, fish it out with the tweezers and dunk it in the glass of cold water. Swish it around to stop the chemical action, then look at it — the shiny aluminum should be corroded to a rich brown-black rust color.

If aluminum color still shows, give the section another quick treatment in the etchant, but be ready to fish it out fast. (The penalty for etching the section too long is that when you go to pull it out, it's not there. You'll lose a few; most kits provide extra corrugated, and Campbell sells the stuff separately, too.)

Now treat the rest of your corrugated stock, a few pieces at a time (if you try to do more than three or four, you'll lose a lot of them). Note: as you work, the chemical reaction heats up the etchant considerably, which makes it work faster. You may want to replace the etchant with cooler solution, or thin it a bit with cold water. Watch out that the etchant doesn't get hot enough to crack the glass — it can.

Change the cold water in the second glass from time to time so that it doesn't become dilute etchant, and remove the treated sections, placing them on paper towel. When you've treated all the aluminum, pour the etchant back in the bottle, carefully wipe up any spilled etchant, and store the bottle where nobody but you can lay hands on it.

Add a few drops of liquid dishwashing detergent to a glass of warm water and thoroughly wash the treated sections, then rinse with more clean water and pat dry with paper towels.

Apply the corrugated as you normally would, but be careful — it's about half the thickness it was before treating it, and easy to crimp or deform! There's some good news, too: the etching gives it some tooth, so it's easier to glue.

You can use this process to eat the corrugated material away until it looks like ultra-weathered "Swiss cheese," and the effect of light filtering through tiny pinholes in the roofing is excellent. BUT, be careful!

DYNA-MODELS SHINGLE ROOFING

Some modelers favor the thin, flexible plastic roof material sold with Dyna-Models kits. Because it's made from a very shiny plastic material most glues and cements won't hold it in place. I've had the best

luck with Elmer's water-soluble contact cement. Follow the instructions on the can for best results.

After the roof is in place it presents some painting problems because of its vinyl-like slickness. I've found two ways that work; Method 1 involves "dry-spraying" Floquil Roof Brown with an airbrush. The paint nozzle should be adjusted so the paint is virtually dry when it hits the roofing. Then streak and highlight the texture with white paint on a stiff-bristled brush.

Method 2 involves coloring the material with brown liquid shoe polish. Make all strokes vertical, and let the polish dry flat. Follow up with a little dry-brushing.

CORNICE RETURNS AND BOXED EAVES

I'm always after a New England look in my modeling, and one way to improve kit structures in this respect is to model the boxed-in eaves and cornice

returns that are so typical of New England frame structures.

The boxed eaves are easy — simply substitute solid stripwood under the eaves for the rafter ends called for in most kits. Real cornice returns call for a little more work, but not much.

Incidentally, if you model New England, most kits have too much roof overhang for New England buildings. Simply trim the gable ends and eaves before you apply the roof to the building, using a photo from your prototype area for reference.

APPLYING CAMPBELL SHINGLES

The gummed brown kraft-paper shingles that have long been part of most Campbell kits are wonderful for simulating the texture of wood-shingled roofs. Yes, they're time-consuming to apply, but the finished effect is top-notch. Here's a handful of hints for applying Campbell shingles:

❶ Do something else at the same time. Watching TV or listening to a ball game on the radio helps alleviate the tedium. Even if it's a good ball game, you can still get an awful lot done during the beer commercials.

❷ Cut several shingle strips to the width of the roof section you're covering and un-curl them with your fingers before you start to apply them.

❸ Use a shot glass to hold the water and a No. 1 watercolor brush to apply it to the upper half of the adhesive on the back of the strip. Then position the strip against the printed guideline on the roof section and poke at the edge with your tweezers to make it meet the line all across the roof. Try placing a scale rule against the lower edge of the shingle strip to force it to straight.

❹ After applying each strip, run the edge of your tweezers along the back edge to push it down firmly against the roof section, then put the roof section aside to dry. Work on at least two roof sections at a time to give individual strips time to dry.

❺ Always make the shingle strips wider than the roof, and when all have dried, trim the section by

placing the edge of a scissors blade under the roof edge and cutting. The scissors I use have a blade just wide enough to leave a neat 2" overhang in HO scale.

MAKING SHAKES FROM CAMPBELL SHINGLES

For a rough, shake-shingle roof effect, trim the length of random individual shingles in each strip before applying it to your roof. This takes a lot of time, and is only worth the effort for foreground buildings.

PAINTING CAMPBELL SHINGLES — TECHNIQUE 1

I've seen numerous buildings with Campbell shingles applied beautifully, then left unpainted. The effect is acceptable, but not nearly as good as you can achieve with some simple coloring.

Method 1 is to stain the completed roof (usually, right on the building) with thinned roof brown paint. Use a mixture of a part paint to 1 part thinner; Floquil railroad colors diluted with Dio-Sol or a flat enamel modeling paint thinned with mineral spirits works best.

When the brown paint dries, lightly dry-brush the roof with light gray or white paint. The dry-brushing highlights the lower edges of the shingles and make them stand out, particularly if you've picked up random bottom edges as suggested above.

PAINTING CAMPBELL SHINGLES — TECHNIQUE 2

This is my favorite way to paint Campbell shingle roofs. I use dirty Floquil Dio-Sol and Flo-Stain wood stains. The Flo-Stain colors are carried in some hobby shops, particularly those that cater to craft hobbyists. I've also found them in art-supply stores.

The Flo-Stain colors I use are Maple, Oak, Driftwood, and a couple of discontinued colors: Silver Spruce Blue and Scotch Pine Green. (If you can't find these last two, make you own by mixing small amount of silver and light blue paints with Dio-Sol for the blue; silver, light green, and Maple for the green.)

Start by wetting the roof section with a large brush dipped in dirty Dio-Sol. Don't get it too wet (I've had styrene windows turn frosty because of fumes inside the building), but apply enough Dio-Sol that the shingles turn dark from the liquid.

While the shingles are wet with the Dio-Sol, randomly apply the Silver Spruce Blue and Scotch Pine

Green stains to various areas of the roof in a splotchy manner. Keep the application uneven.

While the previous colors remain wet, immediately brush on the Maple and Oak stains, straight from

the bottle. Use a fairly large (1/4" wide or wider) brush. Make the coverage haphazard, and don't blend the boundaries between the colors.

Finish the wet-blending with an application of

Driftwood. Use this to work the other colors together, but not too much. Try to eliminate big splotches and streaks, but don't homogenize the color. Let this dry overnight.

Dry-brush the roof sections with Polly S Reefer White or Antique white. I like Antique White for the overall dry-brushing treatment, and Reefer White for a few streaks near the roof peak to represent bird droppings. Don't overdo the droppings, unless you're modeling sea gull territory.

CEDAR SHAKE SHINGLES — THE REAL THING!

One of the oldest ways to make realistic shake shingles, especially in the larger scales, is to use real cedar cigar wrappers. Carefully flatten the wrapper

in the pages of a big book for several days. While you wait, lay out the roof and draw guidelines indicating the placement of the top edges of the shingles.

Cut the thin cedar wrappers into individual shakes (a paper cutter comes in handy for this), and glue to the roof (I like Pliobond here). Start at the bottom edge of the sub-roof and work toward the top.

Coloring is up to you. The cedar can be left as-is for new shakes, or weathered with A-West Weather-It for a silvery, weatherbeaten look.

LETTERING ON THE ROOF

I've added distinctive railroad initials to the roofs of a couple of my stations, and I like the results. Here's how:

First, make sure the roof is dark-colored enough that the lettering will show up. On a roof with

Campbell shingles, for instance, I had to stain the pale tan with a fairly dark mixture of Depot Olive and Grimy Black so there would be some contrast between the roof surface and the yellow lettering.

Next, cut a stencil for the lettering. The best material for the stencil is something clear — artist's drafting Mylar is ideal, but thin clear acetate is just as good. Waxed paper would probably work, too, but make sure you choose something that won't stretch or distort.

Lay out the positions of the letters on the clear material, then burnish down large dry-transfer letters. Use a brand-new No. 10 X-Acto blade (the kind with the rounded edge) to cut out the lettering, being careful to leave "bridges" to parts of letters that would fall out if cut completely ("B," "D," "O," etc.).

Now apply a light coat of rubber cement or something similar (3M No. 77 aerosol multi-purpose spray adhesive is what I use) to the back of the stencil, and let the cement almost dry. The idea is to have enough stickum to hold the stencil to the roof, but to make it dry enough that it won't leave any residue when the stencil is removed. Align the stencil on the roof and gently press it into place.

Mix the paint — Reefer White or Reefer Yellow works best — and airbrush on three almost-dry coats, being careful to spray the paint only at a 90-degree angle to the roof to keep the lettering sharp.

Peel away the stencil, touch up the areas covered by the stencil "bridges" with a brush, and save the stencil for re-use later. ✪

Regardless of the underlying material — wood, brass, plastic, or plaster — what you (and your visitors) see is paint.

8
Painting techniques

PAINT MAKES THE DIFFERENCE in craftsman-style kits, because after all is said and done, what you and your fellow modelers are looking at is a micro-thin layer of paint. I've seen far too many exquisitely assembled craftsman structures that lacked something because the builder's painting techniques weren't as good as his assembly skills.

Painting any kind of material isn't hard if you're willing to work methodically, observe a few basic principles, and above all, take your time. Here are my favorite techniques.

CASTINGS HAVE TO CURE

Window and door castings, either plastic or metal, should be painted early on in your project, then left

> ### Floquil's own thinning formula
>
> Thin full-strength Floquil Railroad Colors for air-brushing by mixing 75% paint with 20% Dio Sol thinner and 5% Glaze. (Glaze is the vehicle — or "stickum" in the paint, and adding it when thinning ensures that the color will flow properly and adhere to the surface being painted.)

to "cure" for a week or more. I like to airbrush castings with Floquil paints, which dry hard — so hard that their own solvent (Dio-Sol) no longer affects them after 7 to 10 days.

PAINT BEFORE ASSEMBLY

Principle No. 1 in building any model, regardless of the material, is to paint as many parts as you can before assembly. There will always be times when you're tempted to forgo pre-painting to get started with the enjoyable business of putting parts together, but you'll invariably save time and effort, as well as come up with better results, if you paint most of the parts before you reach for the glue.

STAINING WOOD SIDING

To give a building that "in-need-of-paint" look so typical of many prototype structures, start by first dipping your brush (a 1/2"-wide one works fine) in thinner, then in full-strength paint, then apply the brush to the siding. Stroke the brush in the same direction as the wood grain and the milled grooves of the siding.

BRUSH PAINTING WOOD WALLS

Moisten wood wall sections with dirty Dio-Sol, and while this is still damp, flow a thinned mix of the Floquil color of your choice over the parts.

Soaking the wood first, then staining, produces a mottled, weathered, and grayed base color which lets the wood texture show through.

STAINING STRIPWOOD WITH A BRUSH

Paint stripwood (after sanding) with a 1/2" brush,

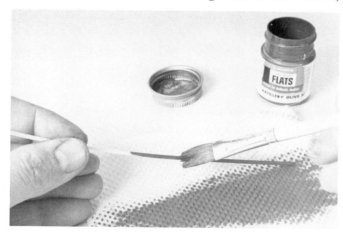

dipping it first into the thinner, then into the paint. Then draw each strip through a scrap of old T-shirt or paper towel moistened with thinner to remove most of the color.

SEALING WOOD AND PAPER

If you have to build models that will be kept in a humid basement or other damp area you already know that all your structures have to be heavily braced. Just as important as bracing is sealing all wood and paper surfaces. I like to use a heavy application (both inside and out) of regular Floquil model railroad paint. Once it's thoroughly dry (that takes at least a week), Floquil becomes impervious — not only to moisture but even to its own thinner, Dio-Sol.

RUB-PAINTING WOOD WITH FLOQUIL

Find an old T-shirt and cut a few swatches about 4" x 6" from it. Fold the swatch into a pad. Dip one corner in the Floquil color you want to use, and rub it, with the grain, on the strip- or sheetwood you want to color. Better yet, draw stripwood through the paint-soaked pad.

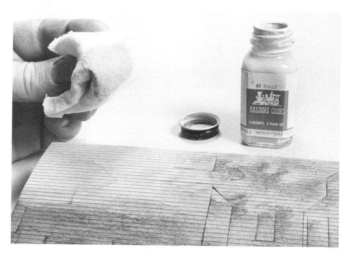

This is an easy way to precisely control the amount of paint applied to wood parts. You can regulate the strength of the tint by dipping the pad in a little Dio-Sol to thin the color.

DULL (BUT REALISTIC) COLORS

A simple way to achieve an overall realistic appearance on a structure (or on your layout) is to dull all colors before applying them to your models. Here's a recipe card:

Formulas for dulling colors

For all colors but white, start by adding 20% white. Strong hues (blues, deep greens, and a few others) may require as much as 30% white.

For white and very light colors, add 10% Earth or some other light tan.

Incidentally, a sure-fire way to employ dull colors, even if you happen to be partially or completely color-blind, is to paint your models with military camouflage colors. Used right out of the bottle, these colors provide pleasingly dull hues.

COLORING WOOD STRUCTURES WITH PASTEL CHALKS

One way to achieve the chalky look of dull, weathered paint is to color wood siding with chalk instead of paint. Start by building walls as subassemblies, but don't install plastic windows or any plastic trim, which should be painted using regular methods. Lay the walls flat and sand them lightly to remove any wood fuzz. Distress the wood with a file card or suede brush, adding board ends, nail holes, and other surface detail.

Seal all the wood surfaces with thinned Floquil

Foundation to eliminate problems with shiny pitch spots. Select the chalk colors you want for the building sides and trim. I prefer the very soft chalks that do not contain wax. To make the chalk stick into a fine powder, rub it over a medium-cut flat bastard file or some coarse sandpaper. Catch the powder on a sheet of paper or in a paper cup.

With a large soft brush (an old shaving brush works fine) pick up a brush load of the powdered chalk and rub it into the walls in the direction of the grain. Blow away the excess chalk powder.

If you have several shades of chalk you can "instantly" weather a building by streaking the walls with rust, dust and faded colors.

Color the trim the same way by brushing individual boards with contrasting chalk. Paint all plastic parts to match the trim.

To seal the powder into the wood, spray the parts with a clear flat finish — I've used Testor's Dullcote, Pactra Clear Flat, and Floquil Flat Finish, all of them work fine. The fixative leaves a little shine, so after it dries dust the walls with some of the leftover powdered chalk to get back to the realistic dead-flat look of weathered (but intact) paint.

DEADENING A COLOR AFTER THE FACT

Suppose you've got an itch to paint a structure a fairly strong color — say, a vibrant blue or a bright green. Trouble is, once you've applied the out-of-the-bottle paint, it comes on too strong.

Don't give up! Instead, try mixing one part of your straight color with one part earth-colored paint. This does the trick, and allows you to use bright colors without overpowering the rest of your layout

CARDBOARD PAINTING AND STORAGE FLATS

For years I've used 12" x 12" scrap corrugated cardboard flats to hold kit parts for painting and storage. Strips of masking tape are fastened, sticky side up, to the flat and cleaned castings stuck to the tape. After spray painting and weathering the parts are used for the kit project at hand or stored on the flat for use later.

Several flats of detail parts, windows, doors, roof brackets, etc. can be prepared ahead of time and stored until needed. If you can't decide what color to paint them, try Floquil Foundation, a neutral beige which is easy to tint or stain to any other color.

PAINTING CASTINGS WITHOUT THE TEDIUM

We all love those kits with dozens upon dozens of detail castings, but sometimes painting all of them can be tedious. Here's a plan of attack that, while it doesn't make it any easier, at least get's the job done painlessly.

Discipline yourself to paint at least one detail part from the kit you're working on any time you open a bottle of paint — for any reason. For instance, say you reach for some Floquil Earth to touch up a raw white plaster spot you've discovered on the layout. While the cap's off the bottle and the brush is dirty, paint at least one casting — preferably several!

USING HARDWARE-STORE PAINTS ON YOUR STRUCTURES

Don't be afraid to try painting your structures using flat paints sold in spray cans in hardware stores. These paints are particularly good on large brick or cement factory-style buildings, especially the Magnuson polyester kits. And, ounce for ounce, they're a bargain compared to hobby paints.

For brick, try Rustoleum Red Primer, Terra Cotta, Gray, or Beige; for concrete, Gray Auto Primer. Allow the paint to dry for an hour or so, then dry-brush the structure lightly with Floquil Rust and Grimy Black.

Follow this with a spray of India ink diluted in rubbing alcohol (1 teaspoon ink to 1 pint of rubbing alcohol), using a hand-pump spray bottle. Spray the sides of the building liberally so the ink-and-alcohol mixture settles into all the cracks and crevices. Allow the building to dry. When the spray dries, dry-brush the surface of the bricks again with a lighter rust color.

Building roofs can be sprayed with any flat dark gray, dark brown or black.

The flat paints are plenty durable, and final weathering can be applied to the finished building using pastel chalk powder or thin washes of Polly S.

GRAY STONE OR CONCRETE COLOR

Here's a formula for a good basic concrete color.

Brush this mix over walls, sidewalks, or foundations. Patterns can be introduced into the concrete by swirling and texturing the paint using a stiff brush.— the stiffer the brush, the rougher the tex-

> **Basic concrete color**
> 3 Parts white flat latex paint
> 1/2 Parts Grumbacher tube-type acrylic gray
> 1 Part Matte Medium

ture. If you want even more texture, add small amount of matte medium. If the results are not as flat as you like omit the matte medium and add 1/2 part talcum powder. Mix well.

FLAT VARNISH FOR TOUCHING UP

One of the last steps before placing a structure on the layout is to look it over for painting imperfections. The most common are shiny spots, which detract from the dead flat look were after. This is easily remedied with a brush and some Testor's Dullcote. Brush on a thin coat, wait until it dries, and evaluate the results in a strong light.

THINNING DULLCOTE

Years ago you could only obtain Testor's Dullcote in spray cans, which were hard to control. In fact, a lot of us used to decant Dullcote from the spray can into a bottle so we could spray it with a regular airbrush. The consistency was just about right.

Nowadays Dullcote is offered in a bottle, but it's too thick for airbrushing. Mix equal parts of bottled Dullcote and lacquer thinner for best airbrushing results; if the finish isn't dead flat, add small quantities of Dullcote until you have what you like.

THINNING ACRYLIC PAINTS

The new Tamiya acrylic paints have their own expensive thinner, but one alternative to it is to use automobile windshield-washer solvent, the stuff that costs $1.69 a gallon. Don't return the thinned paint to the original bottle; instead, keep it in a separate container.

Even if you decide to use the expensive Tamiya solvent for thinning (it's never a bad idea to follow a paint manufacturer's instructions!), the windshield-washer solvent is handy for cleaning brushes and airbrushes — and a darned sight cheaper than a couple of bucks an ounce!

THINNING POLLY S FOR AIRBRUSHING

Polly S colors thin and clean up with water, but to thin them for airbrushing, try a solvent mixture of half water and half rubbing alcohol. It's worth while to make up a bottle of this solvent so you don't have to mix it every time you reach for your airbrush.

PAINTING PLASTIC STRUCTURES

Plastic castings must be clean and free from mold release agents before painting.

Wash the parts with water and liquid dishwashing detergent and rinse thoroughly. Follow this with a quick soaking in denatured alcohol, a wipe with a soft cloth, then allow the parts to air dry. Don't touch the parts with your fingers after this cleaning or you'll foul the surface with skin oils.

If you plan to brush paint the castings, prime them with medium gray. If, instead, you want to stain the parts, prime them with either Floquil RR84 Foundation or RR81 Earth. Allow this base coat to dry a week or more; after a week the paint becomes impervious to its own thinner, and you can stain, overpaint, or weather it without worrying about the solvents eating through the base color.

PAINTING PLASTIC CEDAR SHINGLE ROOFS

Clean the plastic parts with alcohol to remove residues of silicone mold-release compounds. When dry, brush paint with Polly S mixed to a light mud-brown or airbrush with Floquil colors mixed to the same shade.

Allow this base coat to dry overnight (a week, if you can stand it), then heavily dry-brush the shingle tips with Floquil Earth. Add washes of brown, black

and green (for moss) tube-type watercolors to weather the surface. Apply the watercolors by streaking them down the roof.

After the building is assembled, lightly dry-brush the tips of the shingles with Polly S Antique White to highlight the molded-in texture.

PAINTING PLASTIC MASONRY BUILDINGS

Mass-produced plastic kits, where so much of the work is done for you, should come in for lots of care in painting and finishing. One way to approach buildings with brick or stone texture is to airbrush all parts with Floquil colors identical to the colors the parts are cast in. Then rub tube-type oil colors into the mortar lines of the brickwork and stone facings to accentuate the exquisite molded-in relief.

After assembly, use water colors to white out individual bricks, add streaks of weathering, and pick out interesting details.

A QUICKY PAINT JOB FOR PLASTIC BUILDINGS

In a hurry? Try this. Assemble the kit first, except for the window glazing, then spray with Testor's Dullcote from an aerosol can. Let dry a couple of

hours, then paint the trim a contrasting color. Last, dry-brush the structure with Polly S Reefer White to bring out detail and surface texture, and add the clear window material.

COLORING STRATHMORE BOARD

Strathmore is best colored after scribing but while still flat on the workbench. I use a variety of of coloring materials: artists transparent Magic Markers (available in art supply and stationery stores), thinned model railroad paint rubbed on with a soft cloth, dirty paint thinner, and Floquil's Flo-Stains. The object is to keep the coloring thin so it won't obscure any of the surface detail.

If you opt for the Floquil method here's what to do. Prime the cardstock while the Strathmore is still flat on the drawing table before the trim is added. Use dirty Dio-Sol (the stuff that hundreds of brushes have been cleaned in). Swab this on the Strathmore surface. The dirty thinner renders the paper surface a little less thirsty and provides enough pigmentation to show up board separations and grain detail.

While the Dio-Sol is still damp, wipe on your base color with a piece of old T-shirt. Wipe the paint on with the grain of the building siding. If you apply too much paint, dip the T-shirt into clean Dio-Sol and rub away some of the color. Keep alternating between paint and thinner until you achieve the degree of coloring you like.

PAINTING SCALE FURNITURE

Use this two-step procedure to make cast-metal or plastic furniture look like stained wood. First remove flash and assemble the furniture. Dip the finished items in denatured alcohol to remove finger oils. Allow to dry, then spray paint with Floquil Mud.

The Mud colors the furniture a raw wood hue; let it dry completely for a week or so, then stain the furniture using Floquil Flo-Stain or other wood stain colors.

COLORING PRINTED SIGNS

It makes sense to add extra color to printed structure signs while they are flat on the workbench, before they are added to your structure. I use Magic Markers, artist's Hi-Liter coloring pens, transparent

markers, and alcohol dyes to change the sign color. Don't forget to color the edges of signs with a dark brown or black felt-tip pen. As a final touch, deaden the printed surface with powdered pastel chalks.

THE TOP DRY-BRUSHING BRUSH

I like to use a Grumbacher 626-B No. 4 brush for dry-brushing — in fact, over the years I've gone through several dozen of them! This flat, chisel-pointed camel-hair watercolor brush is just right for keeping the dry-brushed color exactly where you want it. These brushes aren't cheap, but you'll be wise to buy two or even three of them at a time, since dry-brushing is really tough on the brush hairs, and they wear down quickly.

CARING FOR YOUR GOOD PAINT BRUSHES

Clean, soft paint brushes last longer and apply paint better than brushes not cared for. It makes no sense to invest several dollars in a fine brush and then have to throw it away after a few uses because it's become hard or misshapen.

Here are three easy steps to good brush care:

❶ After using a brush, clean it first in your everyday dirty thinner, then rinse again in clean thinner. This two-step process removes most of the paint from the brush hairs.

❷ Wash the brush with warm water and soap (you can buy commercial artist's brush soaps, but plain shampoo also works great). Rinse with clear water, and dry the brush, using either an old fabric towel or paper towels.

❸ Finish by working a drop of hair conditioner into the bristles and mold them to the brush's original shape. Then store your brushes upright in a coffee can or Styrofoam block so nothing can deform the hairs.

This simple brush-care drill will take a couple of minutes per brush each time you use it, but I've got 10-year-old brushes in good shape to prove that the routine is well worth the effort.

STORING AND PRESERVING DECALS

Decals are a lot like bread — if you leave them out in the air too long they become stale. Stale decals are hard or impossible to apply; often they just fall apart because the clear carrier film has become brittle and fractured.

To preserve them, store decals in a tightly sealed Ziplock or Daisy seal-a-meal bag, and keep them where the temperature and humidity don't change a lot over the course of the year (for most of us, that's the basement). I've got 10-year-old custom-made decals that are still good as new.

SAVING YOUR PAINT

Over the years I've had a lot of trouble with model paints going sour in the bottle for no apparent reason. This gets expensive, especially when you've got dozens of bottles in your inventory.

This advice pertains to most model paints, but especially to Floquil's Railroad Colors and the Flo-Paque line (it's the same paint). Any paint's biggest foe is air. Most of the brands we use are designed to form a hard, tough film when exposed to air, which either allows the solvent to evaporate, or provides the catalyst for a chemical reaction. This means if there's air in the bottle when you put the paint away, one of the ingredients for making the paint go solid is right there, ready to make the bottle into a clinker the next time you reach for it.

Here's how to save your paint:

❶ When you open a bottle of paint, keep it covered as much as possible during use. Even setting the cap loosely on the bottle helps prevent the solvent from evaporating and keeps the damaging air away.

❷ Before putting the paint away after use, add a few drops of thinner to the bottle, but don't stir or shake the thinner into the paint: Allow it to float on top, helping to protect the paint from the air in the bottle.

❸ Before you re-seal the paint bottle, wipe the neck and the inside rim of the cap with a rag, removing paint residue. Then moisten the rim of the bottle with white glue (to provide a good seal), and screw the cap down tight.

❹ When the bottle gets half empty, pour the remaining paint into a smaller bottle. Floquil sells 5/8-ounce and 1/2-ounce bottles which work well for this.

❺ Write to the manufacturer or distributor of your favorite paint and ask if they sell extra caps and seals. Buy a few dozen, and when a seal becomes torn or the cap is deformed or loaded up with dried paint, replace it. Most paint manufacturers don't list the caps and seals in their catalog, but will sell them to you if you write to ask.

By the way, Floquil adds that once their paint has begun to polymerize, none of the methods described above will stop it.

THE PAINT BOTTLE FACTORY

With a little elbow grease you can have an almost limitless supply of paint bottles. When you empty a glass paint bottle wipe it out with a swatch of paper towel and drop it into a large, wide-mouth bottle filled with half Lestoil and half water. Leave it there for at least a week — what works best is to leave it there until you feel like cleaning out a dozen or more of the bottles.

When you get the bottle-washing urge, wear rubber gloves (Lestoil is strong stuff!) and scrub out the insides of the bottles with an old toothbrush. Rinse thoroughly with hot water, then put the bottles through a cycle in the dishwasher.

Buy new caps and seals from the manufacturer (see the previous hint on saving your paint), and you have a supply of paint bottles for the cost of a bottle of Lestoil. Just keep adding bottles to the Lestoil. Don't throw it out just because it looks bad — in spite of the rugged appearance, it will still work just fine. ✪

Weathering won't cover up bad modeling, but it can enhance even the best construction and finishing.

9

Weathering techniques and formulas

YOU WON'T FIND ME ARGUING about "whether to weather" — since the 1950s I've been weathering all my models with a variety of techniques. If realism is what you're after in your structures, then weathering is a must, simply because everything the real world includes ample evidence of dirt, grime, rain, and yes — weather!

That doesn't mean everything on your layout should be finished to look as though it's on its last legs, or that the same type or degree of weathering should be applied to every structure you build. In fact, having some new, freshly painted buildings here and there will make the run-down ones look all the more convincing by providing a contrast.

There's no right or wrong way to weather models, and most of the methods I use are the result of experimentation, often by others who have published their ideas in magazines. I'll try to give them credit as I mention their techniques below.

UNDERSTANDING WEATHERING

Before you start applying any weathering treatment to your models, take a moment or two to understand what weathering does to things in the real world, and how it occurs. There are really three separate weathering processes: dirt and water, paint fading and failure, and structural failure.

Dirt and water cause most of the effects we want to apply, especially to already-completed models. There are all kinds of dirt, including soil, lubricants, spilled cargo, smoke, soot, and even rust. Water (and sometimes, wind) redistributes dirt, usually causing vertical streaks.

Paint takes a beating when it's exposed to the effects of sun, water, wind, heat, and cold. First the colors fade, then the coating begins to break down, and finally the paint falls away from the surface it was supposed to protect.

Once the protective coating breaks down, the next step is structural failure. Wood dries out and cracks, water makes it rot, and the sun may bleach it; iron and steel rust. Eventually the structure deteriorates to the point where it becomes unserviceable.

The main point is this: You should never apply a weathering treatment to a model unless you can explain to yourself what effect you're trying to achieve with it. For example, when you apply a black or dark-brown wash to something, you know you're simulating the built-up effect of dirt; when you lighten colors with white, you know it's to represent faded paint. And, when you distress wood siding to deepen and emphasize the wood grain, you know it's to model the effects of missing paint and structural failure.

As long as you understand what your weathering is supposed to represent, chances are good that your models will be more — not less — convincing as a result of your weathering efforts.

BASIC PASTEL-CHALK WEATHERING

I first learned about weathering with pastels in a *Model Railroader* article by John Allen way back in 1955. Pastel weathering is probably the easiest technique to learn, the most forgiving, and without a doubt the most subtle. The main ingredient — in fact, about the only ingredient — is a starter set of artist's pastels. One box, which retails for around

four dollars, will probably last at least one lifetime.

We're going to use earth-colored chalk powders to represent dirt, and that's appropriate, because most of the earth colors are simply finely-ground dirt mixed with a binder and formed into a stick. The first step is to grind the chalk into powder, either by rubbing the stick against a coarse file or a swatch of 60-grit sandpaper.

Brush lots of the powder onto the model with a soft brush. Use up-and-down brush strokes to simulate the effects of rain and gravity on the dirt. Use several colors, but always keep a real-world effect in mind, and be sure to make one color predominate. If you think you've applied too much chalk, brush most of it away, but be careful not to leave fingerprints in the dust coating.

Fingerprints are the reason for what we do next. When you have the chalk powder pushed around where you want it, fix it in place with a light spray of a clear flat finish. My favorite is Testor's Dullcote.

Disaster! The clear spray makes most of the chalk disappear! That's one reason pastels are so subtle and controllable. Examine what's left — it may well be an effect you like, but if it isn't, apply more chalk, then more clear fixative spray. Few sprays dry absolutely flat, so before placing the building on your layout give it a final light dusting with chalk, then keep your hands off!

One simple variation on this basic chalk technique is to go over the dusted model with a brush moistened in "wet water" (add a drop or two of liquid dishwashing detergent or Kodak Photo-Flo to a cup of water) to add rain streaks and redistribute the "dirt."

HOW TO DRY-BRUSH

Dry-brushing highlights texture and detail, rendering both more visible. While this technique can

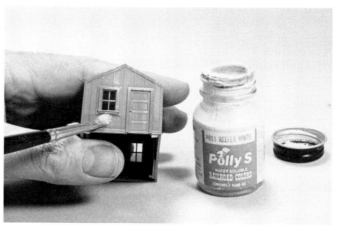

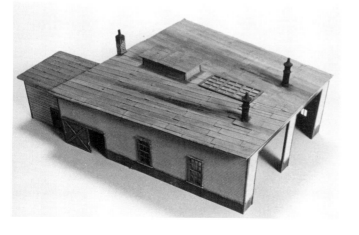

be used to simulate fading and failing paint, I like to think of it as "brushing on sunlight." Dry-brushing improves the look of structures greatly, especially in the low lighting typical of so many layouts.

I use Polly S paints for dry-brushing, for two reasons. First, Polly S is water-based, which means it won't lift or damage the paint it's applied over, no matter how hard you scrub. Second, Polly S is a fairly thick paint, which is best for dry-brushing. The best colors are Antique White, Reefer White, Earth, and Rust, although others are appropriate for representing spilled lading.

The best brush for dry-brushing is a relatively stiff flat watercolor brush about 1/4" wide. My favorite is a Grumbacher style 626-B, and the size is No. 4.

Start by dipping only the tips of the brush hairs in the paint; often I use the paint that sticks to the bottom of the cap instead of dipping the brush into the bottle. Work most of the paint out of the brush by stroking it across a rag, paper towel, or your hand (another reason to use Polly S!).

When all but the last traces of paint have been removed and the brush is "dry," stroke it lightly across the surface of the model, using vertical strokes. Touch the brush to the surface only on the down strokes, so that you deposit paint only on the top edges of raised detail, highlighting them. As the paint disappears from the bristles you'll have to scrub harder and harder to deposit paint on the model.

It's easy to go too far with dry-brushing, so stop before you think you should. You can build up heavier applications of paint to make streaks of bird droppings, rust, soot, or cargo, but until you become comfortable with the technique it's best to quit while you're ahead.

EASY WASH WEATHERING

To give a structure a "painted in" seasoned look, paint it with the color you like, to which you've mixed about 20% white. The white will lighten and dull the color.

After the paint has dried (at least overnight, a week is better), go over the walls with a wash of lamp black (or black pigmented wiping stain, or flat black enamel) thinned with mineral spirits (1/4 teaspoon lamp black to 5 ounces of thinner). This wash fills the nail holes and wood grain with a dark, "grime" color. As the wash starts to dry, go over individual boards with a small brush dipped in clean thinner (Dio-sol if you've used Floquil paints) to blend the dark wash with the base color. This varies the weathering from board to board.

DRY-BRUSHING WALL SUBASSEMBLIES

After wall subassemblies are complete with window and door castings, but before installing window glazing, try lightly dry-brushing the trim and castings with the wall color to make the building "hang together." I use a Grumbacher No. 626B, size 4, which is about 1/4" wide. Dip it into the paint, brush most of the paint off on a pad of paper towel, and

when the brush tips are just about dry, stroke it up and down on the walls and castings. The idea is to leave only traces of color on the uppermost surfaces.

BASICS OF STAINS AND WASHES

If dry-brushing is a way to bring out texture and detail by lightening and highlighting it, stains and washes are means by which we can accomplish the opposite — by darkening and deepening grooves, recesses, and shadows.

You can use any kind of paint to make stains and washes, but may favorites are flat enamels such as Testor's, Pactra, or Humbrol, thinned with mineral spirits. This combination yields washes with very low surface tension, meaning they'll flow readily across the surface of the model and get down into all the nooks and crannies.

The proportion of paint to thinner is not critical,

just be sure to use lots of thinner, as much as 20 or even 50 parts thinner to paint. Most washes are dark colors — brown or black — but occasionally I use a light wash on a dark-colored model.

Apply the wash to the model copiously, allowing it to run into and settle in cracks and around details. If the wash alters the color of the model too much for you, wipe the surface with a clean rag, or brush away the excess color with a clean brush. Then let dry.

Use heavier washes to simulate oil spills or stains left by other liquid cargo, and to represent heavy accumulations of oily dirt and grime.

BASIC WEATHERING FOR WOOD SIDING

Start by diluting paint (Floquil or enamel) with a small amount of thinner, then gray the colors with a little gray paint. Brush the dilute grayed colors over

the wood, let dry 30 seconds, then wipe away most of the paint with a soft cloth (a piece of old T-shirt works best). You can achieve a streaked effect by varying the amount of rubbing you do with the cloth.

Spray paint door and window castings and other trim with another grayed color. Over-spray the completed building VERY lightly with thinned Floquil Dust, then dry-brush highlights (including shingle edges) with Polly S White or Antique White.

HEAVY WEATHERING FOR WOOD SIDING

Wood scribed siding can be painted or stained using all the usual methods, but there's another method that I like to use occasionally for a really run-down building.

Brush dirty Dio-Sol paint thinner on the walls, working only on one side at a time. Don't allow the thinner to dry. While the wood remains wet, brush pastel chalk powder onto it with a large soft brush, working from top to bottom. Different shades of powder produce different effects. I add a lot of white talcum powder and black powder to the chalks to give them a gray, "dusty" look.

The dirty thinner colors the wood and the chalk sticks to the thinner like badly aged paint.

To add shadows under the eaves, add more black to the chalk mix for that area; to show the effects of

water damage or rust, streak green or brown powder down the sides.

Evaluate the colors after the thinner has dried, and brush away excess chalk powder. Once dry, other weathering treatments can be added over the chalks.

DISTRESSING WOOD WITH A FILE CARD

Built-in structural weathering is often the most realistic. Soft wood like balsa, white pine, and basswood can be distressed before they are painted. Balsa works best when you want to simulate really rough wood, like harbor pilings, or tree bark. Distressing adds grain, surface texture and the signs of "wear and tear."

To model deeply distressed wood, such as pier pilings, nothing works quite as well as a file card. This is a special brush with extremely short and stiff bristles, intended for cleaning metal particles from between the teeth of a file (ask for it at your hardware store). Stroke the file card lengthwise along the wood to add deep grain detail. Adjust the pressure for each surface. With practice you'll get it just right, don't overdo it.

Follow up the file card with a finer, brass-bristled suede brush to remove the fuzzies raised by the file card. Then stain and dry-brush.

DISTRESSING SCRIBED SIDING

Use a brass-bristled suede brush to add moderate wood grain relief to scribed siding. Brush with the direction of the milled grooves and the grain. Bear down until the grain looks right.

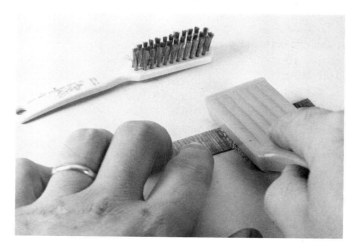

Light sanding will remove any wood fuzz or try burning the fuzz away with a few light strokes of a propane torch flame. Brush the scribed siding lightly to remove dust or loose fuzzies before painting or staining.

ALCOHOL-BASED WOOD STAINS

A fellow named Arnold Crell came up with one of the all-time best techniques in the May 1962 *Model*

Railroader. He diluted shoe dye (not shoe polish, but shoe dye, available at shoe-repair shops), an aniline dye, with denatured alcohol (shellac thinner). The result is an excellent all-purpose, quick-drying wood stain.

You'll need one bottle each of brown and black shoe dye, a pint of denatured alcohol, and some tall bottles with good seals. By varying the proportions of the two dye colors and the alcohol you can come up with an infinite variety of wood tones, but here are three good ones:

Alcohol stains for wood

BASIC BLACK STAIN

      70 drops black shoe dye

      2 oz. Denatured alcohol

BASIC BROWN STAIN

      60 drops brown shoe dye

      2 oz. Denatured alcohol

ALL-PURPOSE WEATHERED WOOD STAIN

      1 part Brown Stain

      2 parts Black Stain

If you want to be really adventurous, try coloring wood siding and trim with some of the colored shoe dyes — but you're on your own here!

DR. WESOLOWSKI'S WEATHERING GOOP

The September 1977 issue of *Railroad Model Craftsman* included an article by well-known modeler Wayne Wesolowski on his all-purpose weathering toner.

The toner consists of one part black leather dye thinned with 15 to 20 parts isopropyl (rubbing) alcohol. Wayne says to use the cheap rubbing alcohol (70%), or to add water to the more-expensive kind (91%) so it's about the same.

An important aspect of using this goop is that after mixing it up once, you don't shake or stir it again.

Instead, Wayne allows the toner to "stratify" — the deeper, darker goop settles to the bottom of the bottle. That way, the deeper you dip your brush into the bottle, the thicker (and stronger) the toner you'll get.

To use the goop, brush it liberally over either finished models or unassembled parts, then allow to dry. A single application of fairly thin toner from the top of the bottle will simply gray down the model; repeated applications will build up darker tones.

SWEET N' SOUR WEATHERING SOLUTION

Yet another innovative approach to workbench chemistry comes from Dwayne Easterling and Jim Wild. Writing in the January 1986 issue of *Railroad Model Craftsman*, they described how they weather wood and plaster with a solution of steel wool dissolved in vinegar.

Making the solution is easy: Start with a one-pint bottle of white salad vinegar, add one pad of steel wool to it, loosen the cap, and let it "work" for about a week.

To apply the solution to stripwood, brush it onto a sheet of glass and place the stripwood on top of it, then brush on more solution. The glass helps keep the wood from warping while the solution dries. When it does, the wood will take on a light red tone; repeated applications will build up darker colors. If you keep air away from the wood as it dries by leaving one side in contact with the glass, you'll get a nice steel-gray color instead.

Brushing the sweet n' sour solution on plaster yields a reddish color appropriate for bricks.

MUD SPATTERS ON STRUCTURE BASES

A fine airbrushed spray of Floquil Mud or Earth where the structure meets the ground does a good job of simulating dirt kicked up onto the sides of the building by rain falling off the eaves. Two constraints: Don't use this effect on every building, and use it only on buildings without conspicuous gutters and downspouts. Choose the color so that the mud spatters match the surrounding earth colors on your layout.

UNDERPAINTING

No, this isn't a technique you apply in your skivvies! The idea with underpainting is that you apply one color, let it dry thoroughly, then apply a second color over it. While the second color is still "soft," you use a brush moistened in thinner to gradually remove it, allowing the base coat to show through.

A typical application is to paint a wood wall gray, let it dry, then paint a second color over it. By selectively removing the upper color you allow the gray to show through, yielding the effect of failing paint with gray weathered wood where the paint has disappeared.

UNDERPAINTING WOOD SHEATHING

Start by brushing individual siding boards with out-of-the-bottle Floquil colors, including every color you have that is even vaguely related to your finished color. For red this means rust, pink, caboose red, boxcar red, roof brown, Tuscan red, — even purple. Let these underneath colors set up for an hour or so before covering them with a thin coat of the desired color. Next, use a brush dampened in Dio-Sol to gradually remove the overcoat and let the underlying colors show through.

The essential feature of this technique is that you are gradually lifting paint and blending the colors to produce a bleached, multicolored variation on the top color. If your result looks a little "striped," subsequent washes and some light dry-brushing will blend it all together.

POUNCE WHEELS FOR NAIL-HOLE DETAIL

Seamstresses use pounce wheels to transfer paper patterns to fabric; the wheel punches dozens of tiny holes through the pattern, then chalk powder is worked through the perforations to transfer the pat-

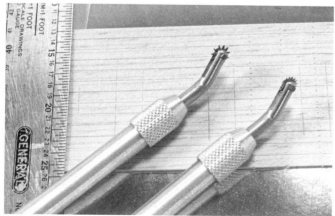

tern to the material in the form of dots.

The same tool does a great job of quickly indenting hundreds of nail holes in wood siding. Line up the row of holes with a steel scale ruler, then roll the

wheel down the side of the wall, leaving a neat row of holes. The wheels come in a variety of sizes — the 15 and 21 holes per inch ones are best for modeling.

If you don't want to be seen at the fabric store, Vintage Reproductions offers a set of "rivet embossing tools" which work fine — and they look like pounce wheels to me!

THE MANY COLORS OF RUST

Rust is everywhere, and it comes in many, many colors. Fresh rust is indeed the bright red-orange of Floquil and Polly S Rust, but older weathered metal turns progressively darker shades of brown, often approaching Roof Brown.

Keep this in mind, and if you have to choose, go for darker rust colors. One of my favorites is Flo-Paque No. F-73 Terra Cotta, an orange-brown that changes to a deeper brown as it dries.

WEATHERING BY REMOVING COLOR

Try this: airbrush a model with thick dirty thinner, then brush away most of the grime with a brush

moistened in clean thinner. The result is an authentic grimy look that makes the model look like it belongs in a grubby industrial district — or a railroad yard!

NASH AND GREENBERG'S RUBBER-CEMENT TRICK

Gary Nash and Mic Greenberg published several articles in the *Narrow Gauge & Short Line Gazette* during the 1970s, and even put out a couple of small books. One of their best — and most original — tricks is to apply small blotches of rubber cement to the model, airbrush it with paint, then pick off the rubber cement blotches. The result is a great simulation of peeling and flaking paint.

Paint or stain the model the gray of weathered wood or the orange-red of rusted metal, then use an old paintbrush to dab patches of rubber cement on the model. You can also apply it with a fingertip, or you might even try try flicking on the rubber cement using the bristles of an old toothbrush. Spray-paint the top color, allow it to dry for a few minutes, then remove the rubber cement with a rubber-cement pickup, available at your art-supply store.

DIP WEATHERING FOR LARGE CASTINGS

Large castings, and even some built-up models and subassemblies, can be dip-weathered. Mix a wash of flat black enamel or black wiping stain and mineral spirits in a wide-mouthed jar (a peanut butter jar is

perfect). Make sure the mineral spirits won't effect the paint on the castings.

Dip each casting into the wash, then stand it upright on a piece of paper towel to drain. Most of the wash will run off and be absorbed by the paper towel, but what stays behind will find its way into the nooks and crannies of the model, simulating the grime that the workaday world deposits there.

"DIRT-DUNK" WEATHERING

My friend Malcolm Furlow swears by the following technique, which he calls "dirt-dunking." Fill an old kit box with fine, dry dirt (preferably from the area you're modeling). Place your finished model in the box, then brush and gently rub the dirt over the

model. Brush or blow away the excess dirt, and there you have it — a "dirt-dunked" instant weathering job.

SHINY METAL

Try representing un-rusted or freshly scraped raw metal surfaces by dry-brushing them with silver Rub N' Buff. Rub N' Buff is a wax-based metal-powder paste used in various crafts; you can find it in crafts shops. ✪

10
About adhesives

CRAFTSMAN-TYPE KITS invariably require that we join dissimilar materials, and that means using a variety of adhesives. In the 30-plus years I've been building these kits, adhesives have gotten better and better — first came model airplane cement, then white glue (it's hard to remember life without white glue!), then 24-hour epoxy, then 5-minute epoxy, and finally, today's cyanoacrylate super glues.

Regardless of their manufacturers' claims, no single glue is perfect for all materials and situations. Sometimes we need speed, sometimes strength, sometimes flexibility. The ability to choose and use adhesives turns out to be as essential a modeling skill as cutting and fitting parts.

THE MOST IMPORTANT GLUING HINT

Keeping the glue from marring the surface of the model is hard to do, but it's absolutely vital if you want models you can be proud of. Here are some good ways to prevent glue blobs from showing.

First, never apply glue to the model directly from the contain the glue comes in — the bottle or tube is made for full-scale projects, and will dispense far more glue than you need for model work. Instead, deposit a drop of glue on some disposable surface, like a three-inch by five-inch file card, then dip into the drop with a flat toothpick and use the toothpick to place glue on the model.

WATER-SOLUBLE GLUE GOOPS

All is not lost when a little (or even a lot) of your white or yellow wood glue oozes onto the surface of the model. If you're prepared you'll have a small container of clean water (a shot glass works great), an old No. 4 paintbrush with the bristles worn or cut

down to about two thirds of their original length, and a folded paper towel handy.

Dip the brush into the water, touch it to the paper towel to remove most of the water, and brush away the glue. Then dip the brush in the water again, stroke it against the towel to remove the glue residue, and go back into the water before repeating the cycle.

When you've removed most of the glue, the rest, reduced to a thin film, dries flat. This works especially well with wood parts that have been painted before assembly, but if you scrub hard you can remove the glue so thoroughly that the wood can be stained with thinned paint or other media.

WHITE GLUE FOR EXTRA TIME

Even if you use fast-drying yellow wood glue for most wood kit assembly, it's better to reach for the white glue when the time comes to assemble wall subassemblies into the building shell.

White glue sets up and dries a lot slower than yellow glue, giving you extra time to align and adjust the walls into a straight, square model.

STORING SUPER GLUE

Keep an eye out for sales on super glue at your local discount stores — if the price is good and the glue looks to be in good condition, buy up a bunch, then seal in Zip Lock bags and store in your freezer. Thaw out as needed.

In my damp basement, open bottles of super glue on the workbench don't last very long. Moisture in the air causes the glue to harden in the tube. You can't keep moisture from attacking the glue, but you can slow it down. I store my open super glue inside a small jar with a screw-top lid. To the jar I add several packets of Silica Gel (the stuff packed with camera lenses and other optical and electronic gadgets to keep them dry). The Silica Gel will absorbs moisture after you close the jar, maintaining dry storage for the super glue between uses.

SUPER GLUE FOR REPAIRS

When a glued joint breaks, reach for your super glue. The break provides a perfect hairline seam, and the super glue sets so fast that there's no waiting. Plus, it's so strong that the joint probably won't break again.

USING BAKING SODA WITH SUPER GLUE

Baking soda makes super glue even more super.

The chemical crystalline structure of baking soda reacts with super glue to form a rock-hard joint that sets instantly.

If you don't believe me try this: Inside your next structure, in a corner or under the floor bracing — anywhere you need extra strength — brush a small

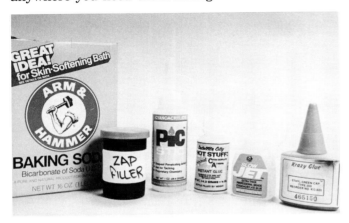

pile of baking soda. Sweep it into the corner you want to reinforce or the crack you want to fill and squirt on several drops of super glue . . . then stand back! The glue is immediately absorbed into the baking powder, heat is generated, and the joint sets rock hard — and it all happens faster than the time it took you to read this.

Super glue and baking soda make great (and strong) interior fillets, and a good gap filler (in fact,

Zap Filler looks like baking soda to me!). Also, when using exceptionally pitchy woods (spruce, and sometimes, sugar pine), a light dusting of baking soda counteracts the pitch and allows the wood to accept the glue.

USING RUBBER CEMENT WITH BUILDING PAPERS

That old standby rubber cement makes a fine addition to your inventory of model building adhesives.

It is a true "contact" cement and should only be used as such. It's not an adhesive that you will use every day, but when you need to join paper to paper or paper to cardstock, it can't be beat.

Try the following procedure several times on scrap walls to get the hang of it before you try rubber cement on a good model. Work with plenty of ventilation!

To glue brick building paper over a cardstock wall, pre-cut the walls to the rough size and draw the final cut lines on the backs of the pieces. Lay the sides on a flat surface and coat the top surfaces evenly with fresh rubber cement (don't use stuff that's been lying around for several years and has gotten thick and goopy). Spread out the building paper and coat its back side with rubber cement.

Allow both coated surfaces to dry so that they are barely sticky to the touch. Lay a piece of waxed paper or newspaper over the building sides and place the building paper on top. Adjust the building paper until it is correctly aligned with the wall, then, while holding the building paper in position slide out the newspaper about 1/2". Smooth the building paper onto the wall of the building. Slide out the newspaper a little more, smooth the building paper against the wall, and repeat the process until all the newspaper has been removed. Be careful not to let the building paper wrinkle while you remove the newspaper because using rubber cement is irreversible, and the paper cannot be removed from the sides..

After the building paper is in place on the walls burnish it in place with the ball of your thumb. The paper should be flat, wrinkle-free, and will adhere to the building side like a glove.

Now the trim the walls and cut openings for doors and windows. Weather the walls with chalks, but be careful with solvent-based paints and washes, as they may dissolve the rubber cement.

THE BEST BRUSHES FOR PLASTIC CEMENT

The applicator brush that comes in bottles of liquid plastic cement is too big for most projects. For tight places where only a little glue is needed, try a No. 0 or 00 round watercolor brush. Wrap tape around the handle to get more brush control and to designate this brush as for cement, not paint.

THINNING PLIOBOND WITH PLASTIC CEMENT

Pliobond (available in most hardware stores) is my favorite adhesive for working with Strathmore board. But as it comes from the bottle, Pliobond is too thick for anything but the crudest work. It has to be thinned.

Here's what to do: when you have about one-quarter inch of Testor's liquid plastic cement left in the bottle, add an equal amount of Pliobond and shake well. As you use the Pliobond just refill the bottle with half plastic cement and half Pliobond.

The liquid plastic cement bottle is a great storage container for thinned Pliobond because it has a brush right in the lid.

MODIFYING STANDARD PLASTIC CEMENT APPLICATORS

Modify the brush on a bottle of Testor's Liquid Plastic Cement by cutting off at least half the length

of the bristles. This lets you apply just the right amount of cement (same as a 00 brush), and because the brush is built into the jar top, it's always handy.

TAPE TIPS

Masking tape is handy stuff for building structures, and not just for masking! One trick that I use often is to place a piece of masking tape on the workbench with the sticky side up. Fasten it in place with two short lengths of tape across the ends. I stick small parts on the tape, then brush or spray paint them without fear of losing them or having them touch other parts.

Masking tape can be used as a clamp to hold identical walls or a bundle of stripwood together while cutting. The tape is also handy as a gluing clamp,

particularly when you need to keep parts in alignment while a slow-setting glue (like epoxy) sets up.

POPSICLE STICKS AS GLUING AIDS

To exert pressure along a length of stripwood trim, use a Popsicle stick. The sticks, available at craft stores for a lot less than we pay for stripwood, also come in handy when the kit instructions call for at-

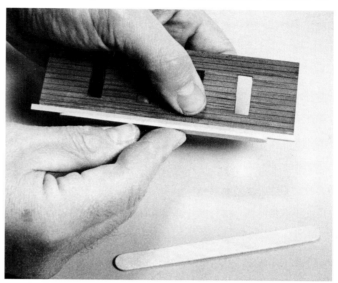

taching a piece of scrap stripwood to the drawing as an alignment aid or stop.

And they make great stirring sticks for our tiny bottles of model paint!

IT'S NOT AN ADHESIVE, BUT . . .

Double-sided carpet tape makes a great paint bottle holder. Stick a short length of the tape on the surface of your workbench, then place your open paint bottle on it. You can still knock the bottle over with your elbow, but it won't be as easy as it usually is. ✪

Chooch's plain-Jane HO General Store comes to life with a few thoughtfully placed details.

11
Tips on detailing

DETAILING IS THE ICING ON THE CAKE for structure models, and although craftsman kits often provide lots of detail parts, it's the work added by the builder — you — that makes the model distinctive and original. Detail doesn't need to be expensive; in fact, some of the most interesting details are free: The main ingredients are your ability to observe the real world and the imagination to incorporate what you see in your modeling.

DETAILING YOUR WAY AROUND MISTAKES

You bet I make mistakes! Always — and most of them stem from not paying attention or not reading the instructions carefully. The trick to overcoming mistakes is simple: Hitch up your pants and forge ahead!

Usually it's a fairly simple trick to recover. When I glue the wrong pieces together, careful prying with the tip of a modeling knife and some steady pressure will usually get them apart. Then a few swipes of a sanding block will remove glue residue and get me back to square one.

Covering up mistakes is easy, once you overcome the pangs of conscience. Downspouts, signs, ladders, even barrels will do the trick. After a while you'll even forget the deception yourself, and think you built the model right in the first place!

INSTALLING CLEAR GLAZING

Regardless of what the instructions say, I try to install clear window glazing as late a possible during construction, so I won't ruin the "glass" with paint. My favorite technique is to thin Pliobond about 25 percent with Testor's liquid plastic cement, then brush on a thin coat around the edges of the window on the inside of the wall. After the Pliobond dries for about a minute and a half, I paint a second thin coat, and press the clear plastic glazing into it. This two-step procedure ensures that the Pliobond won't ooze onto the visible portions of the glazing.

REPLACEMENT GLAZING MATERIAL

A lot of craftsman kits come with clear material for the windows that is far too thin. The flimsy material warps and buckles, and makes odd reflections which don't look real, especially when the building is viewed from outside. Real glass is flat, or nearly so, but trying to simulate it with microscope slide covers, as some have done, is hard, because the thin glass is hard to cut.

One of the best investments you can make is a package of Walthers' No. 949-599 .015" clear styrene. This material is rigid, easy to cut, and easy to glue, and one package is enough for dozens of buildings.

DOUBLE-SIDED TAPE FOR GLAZING

When there's room, use double-sided tape on the inside of the structure to fasten the glazing material. Since you can cut and position pieces of the tape precisely, this material is both fast and neat.

RUBYLITH ART FILM FOR WINDOWS

Rubylith, a graphic-arts material than consists of .005"-thick transparent Mylar with a colored gel attached, has many uses for model building. The first is for protecting window glazing while you paint and weather the model. Cut the Rubylith to the size of the window, remove the red backing, and apply to the film outside surface of the window. After painting remove the Rubylith with a hobby knife and you'll have clean, shiny windows.

Rubylith is also great for modeling scale stained-glass windows, the colored clerestory glass in passenger cars, or anywhere reddish glass is needed. I place it over grain-of-wheat lamps in distant buildings to give that old-time oil lamp look. The film can be crinkled and placed over a light source to model hot coals in a blacksmith's forge.

DIRTY FACTORY WINDOWS

To model windows that would normally be filthy, particularly factory windows, spray them with Testor's Dullcote. This dulls the "glass," rendering it partially non-reflective, and gives the impression of neglect. It also makes it so you can't see inside the structure — and that's good when there's nothing behind those windows.

BACKGROUND WINDOWS

Here are two quick ways to model windows on buildings that will be in the background of your layout:

1. Paint the rear of the clear glazing with Polly S gloss black.

2. Omit the glazing and place a piece of black electrical tape with the sticky side facing out behind the window frame. This is especially good for background structures added just for pictures; if the buildings are permanent, bits of lint and ground foam will eventually stick to the tape, destroying the effect.

BREAK A FEW WINDOWS

I'm not into vandalism, but I often "break" an acetate or clear styrene window to add interest to a

building. After cutting the glazing to size but before adding it to the model, use a sharp modeling knife, and cut a realistic break pattern or cracked spider web into the plastic.

BUT DON'T BREAK EVERYTHING!

We've got to exercise some moderation in the quest for realism. If one crushed 55-gallon drum looks super-realistic, having every drum on your railroad

squashed and rusted should look even more realistic, right? WRONG. The crushed barrel or the broken fence or the swayback boxcar add realism because they present a contrast with the majority of the items in your scenes — as in the real world, most barrels should be intact, most fences in good repair, most boxcars in good condition.

COLORED PAPER WINDOW SHADES

I always add window shades to my structures. They fill the window, give the building a touch of color, and hide most of what's inside the building (in

my structures, usually nothing). When you have fine window mullions, colored paper window shades help point up the fineness.

I use small pieces of green or tan construction paper, the kind kids have in school. The more faded the paper, the more realistic the window shades are. The paper is glued to the rear of the windows after they have been glazed.

OLD WINDOW SHADES

It's hard to achieve the correct color of old, sun-bleached window shades. I found that by soaking strips of white paper in black coffee, then allowing them to dry on paper towels, I could produce a realistic color for older shades. Using different types of paper and altering the strength of the coffee will produce different results.

To use, cut the strips into individual shades with a hobby knife and fasten them behind the windows with white glue.

"FREE" WALLPAPER

The next time a bill comes to your house check the envelope. If its one of those "no-see-through" types with the design printed on the inside, save it. Carefully cut the envelope apart and use the inside pattern for wallpaper in your structures. It may not be

super detail, but it's good enough for HO scale or smaller, and the price is right!

CURTAINS

Colored paper with felt-tip pen marks makes excellent curtains to go behind your window shades. If you have a dwelling right on the front edge of your layout, check the Walthers' catalog for SS Ltd.'s printed curtains and shades.

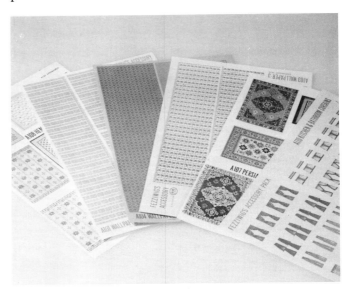

CARDBOARD VIEW BLOCKS INSIDE STRUCTURES

All right, you've installed glazing, shades, and curtains, and you're ready to drop the building into place on your layout. WAIT! Can you look in a front window and see right through, out a back one? Not too realistic, is it?

More than once I've made the mistake of gluing down a structure, only to have to pry it up because it was obvious nothing was inside. The solution is to cut two rectangles of shirt cardboard to run diago-

nally from corner to corner inside the model. Cut a vertical slot halfway across the middle of each piece, and slide them together to make an X- or Y-shaped view block. NOW you can reach for the glue to add the structure to your layout for keeps!

BOLOGNA CUTS FOR FANCY TRIM

Simple milled wood shapes like quarter round can be made into fancy trim for structures by a technique called "bologna slicing." For custom shapes, use either wood or styrene, and carve or sand it to form a long, thin piece with the cross section you need. Then slice the strip — like bologna — with a new single-edge razor blade. Cut at least twice as many bits as you think you'll need. That way, you can choose only the best, most-consistent slices for the model, and discard the rest.

DOORKNOBS

Chuck a brass escutcheon pin in a motor tool and "turn" a doorknob for HO with files. The pin heads

come too big — about 5" across in HO — but turning them down adds a nice detail touch for little work, particularly for foreground buildings or passenger cars.

EASY FIRE ESCAPES

Great-looking fire escapes can be made from brass ladder stock. Straighten the stock and glue or solder two lengths together at right angles. Use the ladder stock as-is to make the connecting ladders.

STRAIGHTENING BRASS GUY WIRES

Every now and then a kit provides semi-curled spring or hard brass wire for making guy wires. It's almost impossible to straighten such wire, and if the guy wires have bows in them they'll look awful.

The solution is to anneal the wire, which relieves the stresses in the metal, leaving it soft and pliable. Carefully heat it in the flame of a propane torch (don't melt it) until it is just red hot. Then withdraw the wire from the flame and allow it to cool slowly in the air. This will leave it soft.

Just before cutting and installing your guy wires, put one end of the annealed wire in a vise, grasp the other end with pliers, and give it a sharp tug. The result will be a perfectly straight length of wire to cut and install.

WHEN IS A DOOR NOT A DOOR?

When it's ajar! Grand Line door castings, and the doors in some kits, provide the door panel separate from the frame. This means you can occasionally

leave a door open (or better yet, slightly ajar), to add a touch of life to the structure and the scene it's in.

Like most other touches, don't apply this tip to every door, or to every structure. Most of us were raised to shut the door behind us!

ADDING GUTTERS AND DOWNSPOUTS

A significant omission in many craftsman kits is the system of gutters and downspouts found on most buildings. Structures in arid regions don't need them, but anywhere it rains they're much in evidence.

The gutters are the hard part: In HO, I most often use Northeastern milled basswood "U" channel, with the outer edges sanded round. Downspouts are easy to make from wire; 1/32" is about right for frame buildings in HO, and bigger structures often have heftier drain pipes. You'll be surprised how much difference the downspouts make to the overall look of the structure; in fact, it's probably worth adding them even without the gutters.

EXTRA CONCRETE TEXTURE

Add extra texture to concrete foundations by brushing on a 50-50 mixture of white glue and water, then sprinkling on fine sand texture material such as John's Lab N scale ballast. When the glue dries completely, give the texture a heavy coat of Polly S gray and streak with black, yellow, and rust to achieve the look of weathered concrete.

AN EASY ROCK FOUNDATION

A simple yet highly detailed foundation can be made from 4-ply Strathmore with individual 2-ply rocks cut out and glued on.

Before setting the structure in place paint each stone a slightly different shade or tint, then mottle the colors together with a unifying wash of gray. Last, streak on white to give a weathered mortar look.

WOOD-BURNING TOOL DETAILING

The granddaddy of all detailing techniques may well be burning texture into the surface of a model. It was popularized by E. L. Moore back in the 1950s and is still used today. It works best on soft woods like balsa, sugar pine, and basswood. The wood-burning tool lets you burn detail into the surface of a model, creating shingles, bricks, flat stones, tile roofing, clapboards, nail holes, and weathering effects such as cracks and worn boards.

Choose a wood-burning tool with a variety of tips. You will not use all the tips but you may need extras to modify for specialty jobs. The Hot Tool mentioned in Chapter 1 is a top-of-line tool, and has numerous uses around the workbench.

FOUNDATION BLOCKS FOR STRUCTURES

I always construct a foundation base in the scenery while I'm building a structure on the workbench. That way, when finished the structure will sit square and level on the layout.

The foundation is nothing more that a flat surface, larger than the base of your building, set level, into the scenery.

You can use any flat material: plywood, Styrofoam, or even heavy cardboard. Some bases can be finished as brick or concrete and left showing to suggest an actual foundation.

Structures can be placed on these blocks at any time during the railroad's construction, and the blocks will ensure that the buildings will be level.

The blocks also allow buildings to be moved around to change the look of the layout.

As I trial fit the structure to the foundation I place

a sheet of clear plastic wrap, the stuff you cover refrigerator dishes with, over the foundation to keep the building from sticking to it.

SIDEWALK AND STREET DETAILS

Use commercial styrene brick sheet to simulate cobblestone streets and brick sidewalks. Don't forget the little details — lamp posts, fire plugs, mailboxes, manhole covers, trash (in and out of cans), and parking meters that make street scenes come alive.

MODELING SIDEWALKS

Sidewalks are normally raised about 4" above the street surface with curbstones 4" wide, 12" deep, and up to 4' long. The width of the sidewalk, from the property line to the street, will vary from one city to another, and from one part of the country to the next, but the general rule of thumb is about 5'.

Early sidewalks were built from cobblestones and brick. After that came poured concrete, then in the early 1950s came asphalt.

The plastic sidewalks that come in Heljan kits are easiest to use. Glue them in place with Walthers' Goo or Pliobond and paint with a 50:50 mixture of Floquil Reefer White and either Earth, Concrete, Grime, Driftwood, or Reefer Gray. The exact color is not important as long as you have a dirty gray-white color, and it will be most realistic if there are subtle variations.

After the paint dries, flow on a light wash made from a few drops of India ink diluted in a pint of rubbing alcohol. Experiment on a piece of scrap sidewalk. The ink/alcohol wash should fill the cracks and crevices with a dark color, but only slightly darken the sidewalk color.

Hide the joint where the sidewalk meets the road by sprinkling fine dirt (to represent sand and gravel), or brown scenic foam (for dead leaves) into the gutter. Glue this in place as follows; spray the gutter with water to moisten the texture material, then follow with a mixture of five parts water to one part white glue, to which a few drops of detergent have been added, applied with an eye dropper.

Sidewalks can also be modeled using poured plaster. Lay scale 4" square pieces of plastic or wood, about four scale feet long, for the curbstone. Form a dike to hold soupy plaster. Glue a square strip on the property side of the sidewalk as the other dike. Paint these the same color gray as the sidewalk will be, and allow the paint to dry.

Spoon soupy plaster between the forms and trowel it level with the edge of a steel ruler. After the plaster sets, lightly sand the sidewalk surface to remove any irregularities, then scribe the joints with a ruler and sharp pencil. Add cracks and broken edges if desired. Paint the sidewalk, then add weeds, grass, and even graffiti.

WATER PUTTY SIDEWALKS

Another quick way to model a poured concrete sidewalk is to glue a flat basswood board where the sidewalk will be. The basswood should be as wide as you want the sidewalk. Over the basswood spread Durham's Rock Hard Water Putty mixed to the consistency of creamy peanut butter. Spread it until

smooth, so it completely covers all the basswood.

Allow it to dry until it just starts to get hard, then, using a sharp scriber and a ruler carve the mortar joints and curbs. Add plenty of cracks and broken sections. When dry, color as described above.

ADD-ONS FOR EXTRA INTEREST

Any building is more interesting if you add "peripherals" to it. Try one or more of these: water tanks, lean-to sheds, free-standing stack, cyclone

dust collector with piping, loading docks, fire escapes, conveyors, and staircases and walkways to the second floor.

SMALL BUILDINGS FOR MORE INTEREST

I have always liked the concept of using many small buildings on a layout instead of a few large ones. Smaller buildings take less space, so you can

put more of them in a given area. Lots of small buildings also help build the illusion of a larger scene, since there's more for the viewer to look at, and the numbers of buildings impress his subconscious inventory of your layout.

Another advantage of little structures is that small buildings don't overpower the trains, so the trains remain the center of interest. I also like small buildings because having them on the layout means I'll have a chance to indulge in more kinds of structures.

ADDING VINES USING RUBBER CEMENT

Rubber cement makes a great adhesive for mounting vines to the sides of buildings. Apply the cement with a small brush. Then sprinkle on green scenic

foam. Use lots of it, and press it into the cement. After it dries for about an hour, shake off the excess, and use a clean brush to flick away excess foam.

Here's the best part: If you don't like how the vine looks on the building, simply rub it away with your thumb. Rubber cement will lift cleanly from most surfaces and roll away.

The exception is printed paper: Rubber cement will lift the ink from most building papers, so be sure to test the cement on building scraps beforehand.

PRINTED SIGNS ON BUILDINGS

Well-known modeler George Sellios showed me how almost any printed sign can be made to look like it was painted on the side of a building. (George is also well known as the proprietor of Fine Scale Miniatures.) Cut out the sign and sand the backing paper away until the paper backing is very thin. Be careful not to make holes in the sign. Take extra care sanding the the edges — they should be so thin you can almost see through them.

Next, carefully weather the sign with a wash of isopropyl alcohol and India ink. Try to match the general weathering on the wall where the sign will be applied. (If you try to weather the sign after it's on the building, the edges will curl.)

When the alcohol wash has dried, brush a thin coating of diluted white glue on the back of the sign and position it on the wall. Rub it down with your fingers to force out air bubbles and excess glue. Mop up any glue that squeezes out with a damp tissue. Last, but most important, use your fingernail to scribe the sign into the horizontal mortar lines of brick or the underneath clapboards. This scribing

step is what makes the sign look like it's painted on, because when the glue dries the sign shrinks onto the wall surface.

As a final touch, blend the sign into the rest of the building by dusting with pastel chalks.

METAL BANDS ON BARRELS

To color the bands on wood barrels quickly and neatly, use a black marking pen with a medium or fine tip. This works for metal or plastic castings.

Start by airbrushing the barrels with Floquil Foundation, let dry several days, then stain with

Flo-Stain. After the stain dries color the bands with a marking pen, then dry-brush with Polly S Antique White. Spots of rust on the bands look good, too.

THREAD FOR TELEGRAPH WIRES AND POWER LINES

I use dark gray or dark green thread for telegraph lines and electrical and phone wires. To remove the fuzz on the thread and add some body to it, run the thread through beeswax until it's glossy. Attach the thread to the insulators with Super-Glue.

MODELING TOMBSTONES

Perhaps because your viewers don't expect to find them, grave markers are real eye-catchers on your layout. Tombstones can be fashioned from bits of wood, carved from plaster blocks or assembled from

leftover plastic kit parts. After you have gathered a dozen or so, weather them with cracks made using a high speed steel bit in a Dremel Moto-Tool.

Paint them to represent blue-gray, green, or pink marble, and add mossy green splotches here and there. Start by priming with off-white, then flow on the final colors as thin stains. Add a few simple crosses made from stripwood, and place your bone yard in the foreground of your layout, where it can be noticed and appreciated. Don't forget vines, weeds, a rusty iron fence, and several clumps of brightly colored flowers.

REMOVABLE ROOFS FOR INTERIOR DETAIL

I once knew a fellow who set out to build a fairly large layout. That's pretty common; what was unusual was that he was so dedicated to interior detailing that he also set out to have a full details inside every structure!

Needless to say, he never accomplished a whole lot, though what he did complete was nothing short of

magnificent. The moral of the story is that interior detailing, like jalapeno peppers, has to be employed in moderation, and then only where you and your visitors can easily see and appreciate it.

Here are my four rules for buildings with removable roofs:

1. Choose your spots carefully. If the model won't be close enough to the edge of the layout for you to easily look straight down into it, forget interior detail.

2. Never worry about the appearance of the underside of the roof. That's not what will draw the attention, so brace the bottom of the roof heavily to prevent warping.

3. Make sure the roof looks good ON the building. Most of the time that's where it will be.

4. Have something going on inside the building. No matter how fancy your furniture or machine tools, the viewer's eye will always be drawn to figures. If you have a feature you particularly want to show off, place a figure close to it.

LIFT-OFF BUILDINGS FOR INTERIOR DETAIL

Making removable roofs is sometimes next to impossible. A worthwhile alternative is to detail the interior but make the entire building — the walls and roof — lift off the base to reveal the inside. This approach means you can glue the roof to the walls for strength, and heavily brace the interior if necessary. It also means you don't have to detail the interior walls if you don't want to — just build up the free-standing interior partitions and furniture, then pop off the whole building to impress your visitors!

FINE SOLDER DETAILS

Fine solder is a much better choice than wire for hoses, cables, other details that have to be coiled or draped realistically. Solder takes paint well, and once you position it, will never change shape.

THE TRAINS RUN PAST THE BACK DOOR, PLEASE!

In most railroad settings, the buildings, especially houses, face away from the track. Oriented as we are to the trains, many of us make the mistake of putting the fronts of buildings facing the track.

Sides and backs are more typical of what you see from the train — the front doors should face the street.

DETAILS FOR THAT SPECIAL TRACKSIDE DWELLING

Foreground houses can include special details: a carved eagle over the front door, white picket fence, carefully trimmed hedges, window boxes with tiny colored flowers, and (for period modelers) a 48-star version of Old Glory on a pole extending out over the porch or standing in the yard.

WEATHERING PEOPLE

A lot of modelers add people to their layout without a thought to how realistic they look. Most out-of-the-box figures have good detail, but you can't see it because of shiny, bright colors.

To bring out the cast-in detail and dull the shine, paint each figure with a dark brown wash. Stand the figure on double-sided tape and paint with a mixture of a few drops of dark brown oil-based stain in a small paint jar full of mineral spirits paint thinner. This should be a thin wash, so that when you brush it on your people it fills in all the crevices without adding a lot of color to the highlights. Adjust the stain by adding more or less stain. For variation try another mixture of lampblack and thinner. Use only oil-base paint thinner such as mineral spirits or turpentine that won't harm plastic figures.

For a final touch you can lightly dry-brush the figures, but keep in mind that this is easy to overdo.

CANVAS ROOF TEXTURE

Single-ply layers of Kleenex soaked in dilute white glue and draped in position make great canvas roofs and awnings. They can be used on old trucks, boxcar roofs, and for awnings, tarps, and tents.

SAVE THOSE TAPE CORES!

The spool-like cores from rolls of Scotch Tape are made from styrene, and are handy for making HO oil or water tanks. I've made several tanks by scrib-

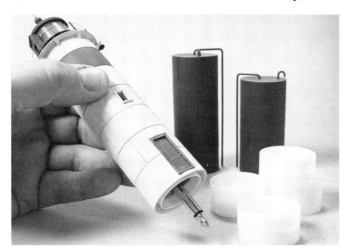

ing two vertical seams across the face of the spool on opposite sides, then stacking several of the cores and adding a flat styrene roof.

Vent and fill pipes made from coat-hanger wire, and a ladder or two from plain old brass ladder stock finish the job. I've even made a steel boiler-plate lighthouse for my harbor scene from tape cores!

SHIPS FOR YOUR HO HARBOR

You won't find many HO ship models, and that's probably OK, since ships are BIG! What you will find are quite a few 1/96 scale models (1/8"=1 foot).

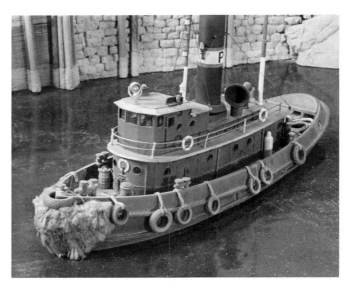

These work well for HO if you make a few changes.

Alter the "people-sized" details, especially the railings, windows, and doors (don't worry about portholes and hatch-type watertight doors; most of them are pretty small anyway). Another "people" detail that establishes scale is life rings, and substituting slightly larger ones, plus painting them bright white or orange, puts across the idea that the model is HO. Finally, figures make the illusion complete.

PRE-WEATHERING PILINGS

Here's how to make realistic weathered pilings for waterfront scenes or trestles. I prefer to cut and

weather them on the workbench, before installing them on the layout.

Start by running a coarse wood rasp up and down the length of a long softwood dowel until it has a cracked, worn appearance. Lightly sand the dowel with coarse sandpaper to remove the fuzz. Cut the pilings to length.

Stain the doweling with a mixture of equal parts black and brown shoe dye diluted with denatured alcohol (see Chapter 9). The dye is absorbed into the wood and dries in a matter of minutes. Over this add your final coloring, weathering, and detailing.

RIGGING TIPS

Running thread through the blocks on a crane, logging hoist, or ship model can be hell. Try these tips:

1. Run the tip of the thread through a drop of

white glue on your fingertip and form the tip to a sharp point.

2. Keep a small weight on one end of the line as you pass it through the sheaves and blocks, to prevent the thread from fouling itself.

3. After all rigging is in place, but before the

longest lines have been glued, put small weights on the ends of the lines to make them taut, and give them a blast of hair spray. When the hair spray dries, glue the lines in place, remove the weights, and the lines should stay taut.

BARNACLES

You won't need this tip unless you're modeling a waterfront scene. Barnacles grow everywhere seawater flows, up to about the high-tide mark. They're small, grayish-white crustaceans that grow to about the size of the tip of your little finger.

To model them start by marking the high tide line.

Hold a pencil on top of a piece of wood and run it all around your waterfront, sliding the block of wood over the water base. The tide line should be no more than nine scale feet above the water surface (unless you're modeling Nova Scotia or some place near the North Pole).

With a small brush paint diluted white glue over the rocks and retaining walls up to the high-tide mark. Sprinkle or "whisk" very fine, off-white ballast (I've used John's Lab No. 504 N scale gray) onto the glue. To "whisk," place the texture material in the "V" of a partially folded 3 x 5 file card and gently blow it into the wet glue. A drinking straw can help to apply and direct the texture if you can't get your face close to the card.

Allow the glue to dry, then brush away the extra barnacles. You can omit the barnacles on areas that will have a heavy covering of seaweed.

Barnacles may be added to pilings before they are installed in the scenery. Brush glue on the pilings up to the high tide mark and dip them in a cup full of the same ballast as used on the scenery. Detail the barnacles by adding clumps of dark blue mussels, some shiny brown seaweed, and other growth. ✦

Index